STRESS

an owner's manual

Arthur Rowshan studied Psychology at the University of Waterloo in Canada, and has taught crisis intervention skills and stress management courses. He now leads his own private consulting firm, offering counselling on stress and chronic pain, with the aid of biofeedback instruments, autogenic training, meditation and guided imagery.

Other self-help books published by Oneworld:

STRESS

an owner's manual

arthur rowshan

ONEWORLD

OXFORD

STRESS
AN OWNER'S MANUAL

Oneworld Publications
(Sales and Editorial)
185 Banbury Road
Oxford OX2 7AR
England

Oneworld Publications
(US Marketing Office)
PO Box 830, 21 Broadway
Rockport, MA 01966
USA

ISBN 1-85168-140-X

Cover design by Peter Maguire
Printed and bound by WSOY, Finland

dedication

This book is dedicated to the memory of my family physician, the late Dr Manoochair Hakim, whose courage and serenity, while persecuted by the Islamic government of Iran, was an inspiration to all of us. Dr Hakim was assassinated in his clinic in 1981 because of his adherence to the Bahá'í Faith.

acknowledgements

Writing a book can be as stressful as giving birth to a child. I was fortunate to have loving and competent people around me who supported me from the 'conception' of the book to its 'delivery'. I would like to express gratitude to the following individuals: my brother Nouri for supporting me in my belief that what I had to write could be useful to others; Dr Victor Rausch, well-known hypnotherapist and stress expert, who granted me his valuable time to discuss health and healing; my clients, who have shared with me their pains and sufferings in dealing with stress; and Jan Nikolic of Oneworld Publications, whose suggestions were instrumental in presenting my ideas clearly and accurately.

contents

PART TWO: four dimensions of stress management

foreword

Psychological stress is one of the most pervasive phenomena of our time and it affects people from all walks of life. Nearly two-thirds of the visits to family physicians in North America are prompted by stress-related problems. Stress is not a modern disease, however; it is a life experience as old as the human species. The term 'stress' was first used in the fifteenth century and has become a household word in our time.

Stress has different meanings for different individuals. To some it is the 'spice of life', while to others it is a scourge to be avoided at all costs. What is stressful to one person may be a source of pleasure for another.

Stress results from the interaction between a person and his or her environment. This environment can be an inner or an outer one. Stress appears when there is a discrepancy between the demands made upon a person and his or her ability to respond to these demands. Individual perceptions of and attitude towards stress have an important bearing on its management. If we can make sense of a life crisis and recognize its relevance to the purpose of our lives, this realization may bring a new understanding that helps us accept the painful event. Cultural values and spiritual insights expand our vision of life events and shape our attitude towards them. Indeed, societal attitudes and values have a powerful influence on our psychological responses to stressors.

In a society where material gain and competitive achievement seem to be the primary purpose of life, and in a culture where happiness is often measured in terms of material success, people have become more dependent on material means as a source of security and power. In such a society, people are more vulnerable to stress, because material attachment cannot bring lasting peace and tranquillity. Therefore, in studying the nature of and response to life stress and crises, we need a broader vision, such as the one offered in this book. We need to evaluate experiences in the light of the psychological, spiritual and physical dimensions of humanity.

Understanding the nature of stress and how human beings adapt to it has important implications for our personal development, because psychological stress can serve as a stimulus or an impediment to personal growth and fulfilment. The effect of stress may not be the same on the same person at various stages of life, nor are the perception and interpretation of stress alike in people of different backgrounds. Thunder and lightning can be a frightening experience for a child, but a farmer will welcome these harbingers of rain for his fields.

Managing stress is an art and life is a workshop in which we master this art and grow in the process. For those who are reluctant to face up to this challenge, stress becomes a source of pain and distress. But those who willingly face the challenge are enriched by the experience.

This book is about mastering the art of coping with stress. It emphasizes the spiritual dimension of adaptation to stress, since stress management is not only a matter of technical skills. The author goes beyond symptoms and addresses the person as a whole. In discussing the vicissitudes of stress, Arthur Rowshan points out the benefits of manageable stress as well as the dangers when it becomes excessive. His approach is simple, pragmatic, informative and enriched by broad personal experience as well as practical examples. The book covers a wide range of stress-related issues, from nutrition to meditation, and from the immune system to goal-setting and communication of feeling. With a creative sense of humour and optimism, the author offers a holistic approach to stress management that particularly emphasizes prevention, and outlines the physical, mental, emotional and spiritual dimensions of human responses to life stress.

Abdu'l-Missagh Ghadirian
Canada

introduction

why I wrote this book

Sam was my first client. He came to me for help with controlling stress. He was a shy and insecure Iranian teenager who
had moved to Italy for his studies. He was living with one of
his brothers in Rome, but felt lonely and depressed. His main
problem was a throbbing headache that he had suffered from for
two years.

He told me that he had tried every possible treatment he could
find to alleviate the pain. He had begun with his family doctor, and
had seen specialists, an acupuncturist and finally a psychologist; he
had taken every drug his doctors had prescribed. Even the strongest
painkillers did not ease his headache.

Only his psychologist had attempted to get past the symptoms to
the cause of the pain. The psychologist's questions made him think
about his situation: he was far from his family, and the Islamic
Revolution had erupted in his native land, a revolution that meant
persecution for his family and other Bahá'ís in Iran. Soon he began to
receive news of his relatives being imprisoned, tortured and hanged.

As I listened to his words and looked into his eyes, I realized
how like me he was. His story was my story. My own experience as

a Bahá'í in Iran for the first sixteen years of my life had left me with many bitter feelings. My schoolmates and teachers treated me as a *'najes'*, that is, an 'untouchable'. I wasn't even allowed in the school cafeteria. When one day I finally managed to sneak in, someone informed the owner. He came up to me and said, 'You are a Bahá'í? Now I have to rinse your glass!' That was my first and last visit to the cafeteria.

I also remember the day I was walking with my cousin when a gang of boys threw rocks at us, calling us 'dirty Bahá'ís'. My brothers were beaten regularly by more fanatical Muslims. And, after the Islamic Revolution in Iran, many of my relatives were imprisoned, tortured and executed for being Bahá'ís. The experience of persecution gave me the motivation to apply many of the teachings of the Bahá'í Faith in regard to stress and suffering.

Since that early meeting with Sam I have become increasingly interested in the study of human behaviour and specifically in psychosomatic illness. Through research and study, observation and interviews, I began to focus on people who were resilient in times of stress, and to investigate their methods of coping. My own newfound ability to deal with stress has led to the writing of this book; it is the result of seven years of intense study and experience in helping myself and others enjoy life more fully by dealing more effectively with the stress of life's challenges.

I offer it to you in the hope that what I have learnt brings you as much peace as it has brought me.

Why an owner's manual

As the title of this book suggests, we must own our stress. This sense of responsibility allows us to have choices about our behaviour. We cannot always control the situation, but are ultimately in charge of our actions. Moreover 'an owner's manual' implies that there is something useful about stress. As you read the book, you will realize that stress is a tremendous force in our lives which can become a source of joy and excitement.

If you are not happy with the way you handle stress, or would like to improve your skill in dealing with it, this book is for you. No matter who you are, you have been and will be faced with the challenges of living. These challenges range from the trivial, like traffic jams, to critical challenges, like the death of loved ones.

Sometimes even a slight change can put us under pressure. Most individuals experience much crisis and growing pains during their adolescent years because the transition from youth to adulthood and maturity is not an easy one. Likewise humanity as a whole is experiencing its most turbulent stage of development. The transition from the twentieth to the twenty-first century has been marked by wars, and by political and economic conflicts. The dizzying pace of the changes of this period of history has become a major source of stress.

My aims in writing the book are twofold: 1) to make you aware of your daily stress; and 2) to help you prevent it, reduce it, and manage it. Awareness is the first step towards improvement. Through daily practice you can learn to live with stress and love it.

how to use what you learn

I recommend that you read this book through once to get a feeling for its structure, then read each chapter at your own pace. I suggest you use a notebook to write down any ideas, quotations and exercises that immediately strike you as useful. Practise each technique for three weeks in order to master it. Repetition is the key to learning.

Your learning process will progress through four stages:

1. unconscious incompetence;
2. conscious incompetence;
3. conscious competence;
4. unconscious competence.

In the first stage you are unaware of your mistakes. You might become frequently irritated, but you remain unconscious of the ineffectiveness of your behaviour.

In the second stage, you begin to realize that you are doing something improperly. You become aware of your poor performance in a specific area, and if you decide to improve, you can change your behaviour.

In the third stage, you will finally isolate a particular skill and commit yourself to practising it. This stage is similar to sitting on a bicycle for the first time and wanting to learn how to ride it. As a parent or friend holds the bicycle, you begin to pedal, check your balance, look at your feet, look in front of you, and go straight ahead. You have to pay conscious attention to all of these necessary procedures. You have to make an effort to follow instructions until you find yourself finally riding the bicycle all by yourself.

Once you learn to ride the bicycle, you no longer think about every single detail. In this last stage of learning a new skill, 'over-learning', you don't need to pay conscious attention to what you do. Pedalling, balancing, and steering become second nature to you, each function happily integrated into the whole set of functions. At this stage, the performance of the skill becomes not only effortless but also fun.

Reading this book is like riding your first bicycle. To be able to master the relaxation techniques or the principles of stress management, you need to practise these skills until you 'overlearn' them. I hope that you will be able to familiarize yourself with the 'bicycle' of stress to the extent that you also enjoy the ride.

PART

one

defining stress

one

its nature
and symptoms

what is stress?

Stress is always with us. Depending on the situation, it varies in intensity. Right now, while you are reading these lines, you are experiencing some stress: you are holding the book open, your eyes are following the words, and you are constantly processing the information you receive. Even if, instead of reading this book, you were lying down in a very relaxed position with your eyes closed, you would still be experiencing stress, because inside your body is another world. As it goes about its complicated functions from moment to moment, your brain is always working, while your heart pumps blood regularly and incessantly, and your lungs alternately empty themselves and fill with air. Therefore, in a technical sense, we all constantly experience stress, because when we are conscious we are always adding to the body's list of things to do.

Contrary to popular belief, stress is not always bad; it can be an effective motivator that adds spice to your life. Olympic athletes do not usually break records during training, nor do actors give their best performances during rehearsals; like every one of us, they are at their best when invigorated by the stress of performing before the eager gaze of a watchful audience.

The Chinese word for crisis is a combination of the symbol for danger and the symbol for opportunity, and stress shares these two ingredients. Every problem has inherent in it its own solution; each time you are under stress, you have the potential for both destructive and constructive use of your energy. A surgeon at work in the operating room is under so much stress that his or her pulse rate goes up by an average of fifty beats per minute. But this is fortunate, since none of us wants to be operated on by a doctor who's too relaxed or easygoing at such a crucial moment! Successful people channel their stress into constructive energy and creative power.

Let's look at the anatomy of stress. Since the stress response is mainly physical, it is important to become familiar with what happens in your body in times of stress.

Imagine that you have travelled back millions of years in time. You are sitting beside the fire in a cave. As you are enjoying your meal, you notice a nearby animal. As you turn your head, a large and ferocious-looking sabre-toothed tiger charges towards you! Immediately your body goes through a series of drastic changes. The essential 'fight-or-flight' response is Mother Nature's way of protecting you from danger. This innate and automatic response is characterized by the following changes in your body:

1. As soon as your brain registers the fact of the tiger's approach, adrenaline is released into your body, bringing about several physical changes.

2. The pupils of your eyes dilate to allow more light in and sharpen your vision. In times of perceived danger you need to see as much as you can.

3. Your mouth goes dry to avoid adding fluid to your stomach.

4. As a consequence, your digestion stops temporarily, allowing more blood to be directed to the muscles and the brain. This explains why in times of stress you feel 'butterflies' in your stomach.

5. Your neck and shoulder muscles tense up in order to prepare for action. Tense muscles are more resilient to blows than relaxed muscles.

6. Your breathing quickens to allow an increased flow of oxygen to your muscles.

7. Your heart beats faster and your blood pressure rises, thereby providing more fuel and oxygen to the various parts of the body.

8. Your perspiration increases in order to cool the body down. The more energy the body burns, the more you perspire.

9. Your liver releases glucose to provide a quick burst of energy for the muscles.

10. Your spleen releases its stored blood cells and chemicals into the blood stream to thicken the blood. This process allows the blood to clot more rapidly than usual, so that if injury should occur, the bleeding will stop more quickly. Moreover, the body becomes more resistant to infection.

These automatic reflex responses to danger are still with us today. Everyday situations can trigger the hypothalamus, or 'stress centre', in our brains to bring about all of the above changes. And the same responses are elicited by a frustrating traffic jam or an angry boss as our ancestors experienced in the bush when encountering a wild animal.

The stress response, then, is our body's preparation for either confronting or fleeing from danger. No matter whether your split-second decision is to fight or to run away, your body will need all the alertness and extra energy it can get.

But in the modern world we pay a price for the mismanagement of this response. Unlike the cave dwellers who either fought or ran, we are often trapped within our stressful predicament without a direct means of addressing it. We do not strike our boss, for instance, no matter how tempted we might be to do so, when angered or frustrated by him or her. Therefore, we do not release the physical tension caused by physiological changes. And when we fail to release this stored tension, we fall victim to a series of stress-related symptoms, such as the following:

1. Chronic pupil dilation, which may bring about vision problems.

2. Excessive dryness of the mouth, which may cause difficulty in swallowing.

3. Too frequent interruptions of the digestive process, which may give rise to constipation or encourage ulcers.

4. Chronic muscle tension, which causes bodily aches and pains, the most common of these being the pain caused by stiff neck or shoulder muscles.

5. Chronic shallow and rapid breathing, which can lead to asthma.

6. Chronic blood pressure increases, which can lead to a permanent state of high blood pressure.

So, no matter what its psychological components, stress always has physiological results. When you perceive a stressor, the hypothalamus releases chemicals that stimulate the pituitary gland to release hormones targeted to the adrenal glands. In turn the adrenal glands release the adrenaline responsible for the drastic physical changes in your body.

It may surprise you to know that your body responds to pleasant and unpleasant events in the same way. Whether you are fired or promoted, slapped in the face or caressed by your lover, arguing with someone or making love to them, your physical response to stress is the same. Any change, positive or negative, brings about the same physiological reactions associated with the fight-or-flight response.

Although our physiological responses to both positive and negative stresses are identical, our interpretation of events can differ greatly. For example, public speaking strikes many people as stressful (North Americans claim it as their number one fear). Yet a select few not only earn their living giving speeches, but also enjoy doing it. The difference is in the way the timid and the self-confident manage their stress.

The mismanaging of our stress response gives rise to a host of problems. The biological reaction that mobilizes our bodily defences – really an act of self-preservation – can be triggered by both real and imaginary dangers. For example, if you were sitting at home enjoying your favourite TV programme, happy and relaxed, and you suddenly remembered that you had left an important project unfinished at work, your breathing would become short and rapid, your heart would race, your muscles would tense up, and your blood pressure would shoot up, perhaps inducing a headache. Although most of our irritating modern-day stressors are not life threatening, the body's automatic physical reactions to them are the same as the ones our ancestors felt when facing a wild animal. Though free from the threat of wild animals prowling in the streets, we nevertheless have deadlines, traffic jams, overdue bills, and 'impossible' people to cause us the same levels of stress.

Your response to stress depends on a number of factors. First, a strong and healthy genetic make-up and lack of any major family diseases (like heart attack and stroke) make you more resilient to stress. Unfortunately, there isn't much you can do about the physical traits you inherit.

The second major factor is parental modelling. The way your parents deal with stress has influenced you – wittingly or unwittingly – in the way you respond to daily irritations. Although we are not carbon copies of our parents, we are very much influenced by their personality and attitudes. If, in your childhood home, you saw pandemonium ensue whenever dinner was burnt, you are likely to react in the same way in a future instance.

Thirdly, your present attitudes, expectations and belief systems, a by-product of your cultural background and education, influence your response to stressors. Again, these major influences on the way we handle stress are not easily escaped from.

symptoms of stress

For any self-development programme to be successful, we need to know three things:

1. Where we are.

2. Where we want to go.

3. How to get there.

A stress self-analysis helps you discover where you are in terms of your way of responding to stress. Becoming aware of the warning signs of stress is the first step towards improvement. Once you become familiar with the signs, you can prevent them from growing into chronic symptoms.

These warning signs fall into five categories: spiritual, social, emotional, mental and physical. You may experience symptoms in all these categories. Moreover, they influence each other, and often they can entrap you in a vicious circle. For example, if your response to a heated argument is to get a headache, the pain may disrupt your sleep, and in turn lack of sleep becomes a stressor affecting your mood. Stress factors are often elaborately – and infuriatingly – interconnected.

Take your time and answer 'yes' or 'no' to the following lists of questions. You may want to read over these lists several times in order to help you remember them. Then when you experience any of these symptoms in times of stress, you will be more aware of them. If you recognize a large number of the signs in yourself, DO NOT PANIC. This means that you are among those who can benefit most from applying the principles and techniques outlined in this book.

Add up the number of ticks in the 'yes' category and look up your score at the end to get an idea of your stress level. There are no 'winners' and 'losers' here, only those who can benefit to a greater or lesser degree from the advice in this book.

Physical Signs

yes / no

Have you recently suffered from a major injury or illness? ☐ ☐

Do you smoke and/or drink heavily? ☐ ☐

Do you have irregular eating habits/an eating disorder? ☐ ☐

Does your weight fluctuate greatly? ☐ ☐

Do you have difficulty sleeping or getting up in the morning? ☐ ☐

Do you feel constantly tired? ☐ ☐

Do you lead a sedentary lifestyle? ☐ ☐

Do you have high blood pressure? ☐ ☐

Do you suffer from frequent colds? ☐ ☐

Do you suffer from constipation or frequent urination? ☐ ☐

Do you suffer from headaches/back pain/other recurrent aches? ☐ ☐

Do you suffer from muscle spasms? ☐ ☐

Do you suffer from stiffness and tension? ☐ ☐

Do you have excessively cold hands and feet? ☐ ☐

Do you have nervous habits (teeth grinding, nail biting, foot tapping, etc.)? ☐ ☐

Do you often tremble? ☐ ☐

Are you often short of breath? ☐ ☐

Do you sweat excessively? ☐ ☐

Do you suffer from indigestion/ulcers? ☐ ☐

Do you have any allergies? ☐ ☐

Do you have abnormal menstrual cycles? ☐ ☐

Do you suffer from dryness of the throat and mouth? ☐ ☐

Social Signs

yes / no

Has a close friend or family member died
recently? ☐ ☐

Have you recently got married or divorced? ☐ ☐

Do you have major arguments with your partner? ☐ ☐

Do you have difficulty asking assertively for
what you want? ☐ ☐

Do you have difficulty saying 'no' to
inappropriate requests? ☐ ☐

Do you have difficulty making decisions? ☐ ☐

Do you feel bitterness/intolerance/jealousy
toward other people? ☐ ☐

Do you get impatient or irritable when people
speak slowly? ☐ ☐

Are you competitive? ☐ ☐

Are you self-centred? ☐ ☐

Have you had an outstanding achievement
recently? ☐ ☐

Is your job too demanding/boring/are you
unemployed? ☐ ☐

Are you unhappy about your financial situation? ☐ ☐

Are you unhappy about your sex life? ☐ ☐

Do you feel like withdrawing from society? ☐ ☐

Emotional Signs

Do you have rapid mood swings? ☐ ☐

Do you get angry easily? ☐ ☐

Do you suffer from anxiety attacks? ☐ ☐

Do you suffer from depression/frequent feelings
of despair? ☐ ☐

Are you a worrier? ☐ ☐

Do you often feel apathetic? ☐ ☐

Do you have frequent nightmares? ☐ ☐

Do you often feel restless? ☐ ☐

Do you often burst into tears? ☐ ☐
Do you often laugh nervously? ☐ ☐
Are you a hypochondriac? ☐ ☐
Do you often feel emotionally numb? ☐ ☐

Mental Signs

Are you often bored? ☐ ☐
Do you become frustrated waiting in queues? ☐ ☐
Do you feel you are always behind schedule? ☐ ☐
Do you feel people don't appreciate you? ☐ ☐
Do you have constant negative self-talk? ☐ ☐
Do you rush things/do several things at the ☐ ☐
  same time?
Do you deny your problems? ☐ ☐
Do you have frequent lapses of memory? ☐ ☐
Do you have difficulty concentrating? ☐ ☐
Do you often feel confused? ☐ ☐
Are you pessimistic? ☐ ☐
Do you have any phobias? ☐ ☐
Do you ever contemplate suicide? ☐ ☐
Is there something you dislike about ☐ ☐
  your body?

Spiritual Signs

Do you feel alone? ☐ ☐
Do you have feelings of emptiness or ☐ ☐
  hopelessness?
Do you find it difficult to forgive? ☐ ☐
Has life lost its meaning for you? ☐ ☐
Do you feel as if you have lost your direction? ☐ ☐
Do you often have guilt feelings? ☐ ☐
Do you feel hostility towards others? ☐ ☐
Do you practise self abuse in any form? ☐ ☐

To find out your score:

Yes: 1 Point   No: 0 Points

0–24: Congratulations! You have a healthy lifestyle.

25–39: Medium stress level. You will benefit from adopting some health habits.

40–71: High stress level (high potential for stress-related illnesses). You could benefit greatly from reflecting on your lifestyle and making significant changes.

How did you do? Now that you have recognized some of the common signs of stress that affect you, take the next step. Ask yourself when you are likely to experience these symptoms. Do you get a stiff neck while working on a difficult project? Do you feel depressed or guilty after an argument with your parents? Once you isolate the situation and events, you can learn to respond differently in those situations when you are likely to experience such symptoms. You may also wish to discuss your symptoms with your family doctor.

the stress response

Although we refer to the stress-inducing event or situation as a 'stressor', it is really more accurate to consider a stressor as something that challenges us in some way. Astonishing stories about soldiers who have found themselves suddenly able to lift a jeep in order to free a friend trapped beneath it can be accounted for by theories of stress. Under very stressful conditions, we all have the potential for extraordinary feats of strength or endurance.

The simplest definition of stress is a *response* to demands. While most people think that stress is caused by what happens to them, in reality it is their *own response* to apparently stressful situations that causes their feelings of tension and anxiety. I explain this phenomenon in my seminars by means of the HERO principle. You might consider the HERO principle whenever you are faced with a potential stressor. According to this principle, there are four aspects to the stress situation:

Happening
Evaluation
Response
Outcome

The Happening is the event or situation that you face at any given moment. The Evaluation of the event involves your attitudes, beliefs and expectations; you interpret the stressor and give meaning to it. The Response (fight-or-flight) is based on your evaluation, and the Outcome is what you cause to happen as a result of your response. Because we only see the outcome, we often think that the happening 'caused' the outcome, but in doing so we overlook our evaluation and response. Understanding this principle allows you to be in charge of your thoughts and actions.

To illustrate the HERO principle, we could take the example of an insult. Someone calls you a name, such as 'stupid'. The insult is the stressor, the 'H' or *happening* of the HERO principle. Now it is your turn: you *evaluate* the insult. You might say to yourself, 'I must've done something wrong to deserve that'. After you give meaning to the event, you *respond*, maybe by tensing up your neck and shoulder muscles, disturbing the flow of blood to your brain. Finally you have the *outcome* of your response, which may in this case be a headache or a stiff neck. When we call troublesome people a 'headache' or 'a pain in the neck', we are often referring rather literally to their effect on us!

The key to the HERO principle is your evaluation of the event. By this means you determine the outcome or the amount of stress that you eventually experience. I don't mean that the stress you experience is all your fault, but rather that your thoughts and attitudes play a crucial role in forming your outlook on what happens to you in life. Since they are *your* thoughts and attitudes, *you* are in charge of them. *You* own them and can control them; for instance, in the example above, you did not have to decide to feel either angry or ashamed at being called 'stupid'.

You can break the vicious circle of stressful response by first reminding yourself that events *per se* are neutral. How you interpret your experiences, what labels you give them, determines how you feel and act. So start by taking charge of your thoughts. *Remember, you may not have control over what happens to you, but you are in charge of how you respond.* Monitor your reactions. When you get angry or get a headache, note what you were thinking just before the flow of unpleasant feelings began. At first you may find it difficult to catch your thoughts in the act, so to speak, and of course a large number of your thoughts lie beyond your conscious awareness. With practice, however, you will be able to catch your negative thoughts and correct them before it's too late. Be persistent and practise.

An Example of the Constructive Use of the HERO Principle

Happening Your boss complains about your performance on a project.

Evaluation You can say to yourself, 'She cares about me. She is giving me feedback on my work. I'll go and ask her what specific things she didn't like about my work'.

Response When you see your boss you can say, 'Could you please explain to me which parts of this project need improvement? I'll be glad to work on the weak points. Would you also tell me the strengths of my project? What are the most effective parts of my work on it so far?' Then thank her for her feedback.

Outcome You feel good about yourself and your job. Your boss is impressed with how well you handled criticism, something that may even figure in a future pay increase or promotion. Most important of all, you retain your self-esteem and self-worth.

You see, *we choose* to behave the way we do. The world around us does not 'make' us do what we do. Your getting angry or remaining calm is your own conscious or unconscious decision. So the stress you experience in your life is entirely under your control. Since you are in charge, generating effective, creative behaviour is just as easy as doing the opposite.

Someone who says 'you make me angry' has forgotten that it's impossible for a human being to create or cause feelings for another human being. We create our own feelings. Instead of 'You make me this way or that', it's more accurate to say 'When you do or say this or that, I feel this'. Don't confuse your own reactions with the actions of others. Once you take responsibility for your own feelings, you will be surprised and pleased at how creatively and constructively you can use them.

styled creative response

Although the fight-or-flight response is our innate biological response to stress, we are not doomed to fall victim to it. Instead, we can face up to the stress by looking for the opportunity that it brings. I learned this principle from my Kung Fu master, and when I was a Kung Fu instructor with my own students, I taught them to practise this philosophy in their training and in their daily life. According to the tenets of this philosophy, you should never confront force with force, but rather you should 'flow' with the force. You position yourself beside the blow, and in this position you are able to change the course of the attack by using its own energy. This flexibility of movement is the essence of the Kung Fu expert's winning strategy.

Our alternative to the fight-or-flight response is what I call 'Styled Creative Response', one that goes beyond the typical reaction to stressors. The word 'styled' suggests not only that your response is your own, but that there is no necessarily right or best way of responding to stressors. Each of us is different, and each of us has a unique approach to life. Adopt the kind of response that suits your personality or self-image. For example, if it suits you, you might use humour to calm your anger. You can also use positive self-talk to manage your emotions effectively. Discover your own behavioural style. You could observe people you admire and trust, and model your own specific behaviour in stressful circumstances after theirs. If you like the *results* of their styled response to stress, then try doing as they do.

The word 'creative' suggests that your behaviour goes beyond the limiting extremes of fight-or-flight. Creativity gives you some latitude of choice in your behaviour, allowing you to react to an insult with unexpected humour, for instance, rather than the more usual anger.

Let me give an example. During my university years I lived in a basement flat. One day, returning from a lecture, I stepped in and heard an ominous splashing sound. When I switched on the light, I discovered that the whole apartment was inundated with water. I became furious as I remembered that the landlord had been lazy and had not got round to fixing a leaking pipe in the ceiling. After a short while the landlord came down with two mops in his hands. I was so upset that I couldn't say a word. He smiled and said, 'Well, at least you don't have to go to Venice now!' His comment took me by surprise since I was expecting the usual apologies or excuses. I couldn't help but laugh too. His humorous comment changed my perception of the situation – from catastrophizing to an opportunity to chuckle. There was really no harm done to me after all, since all the furniture was his and the most precious things, my books, were dry on their shelves.

A study on fear was undertaken in England during the Second World War. During nightly air bombardments in London, when entire neighbourhoods were being destroyed, researchers checked people in the streets for stress and anxiety levels. They also tested people living in the rural areas where there was no bombing. Surprisingly, the rural people showed higher anxiety levels than the city dwellers. Why? Perhaps because the city people accepted the bombings as a regular event and adjusted their lives to cope with them. Meanwhile, the rural people would worry about the possibility of being bombed, and the unpredictability of such a thing caused them much stress and anxiety.

There are many examples of people who in times of suffering and stress respond courageously and creatively. British astrophysicist and Cambridge University mathematics professor Stephen Hawking persevered through the pain and distress of a rare degenerative muscle disease to become the world's foremost mathematician, occupying the chair of Sir Isaac Newton himself. Dick York, star of the television series *Bewitched*, suffers from emphysema, a debilitating lung disease. Despite the fact that he is housebound most of the time, York manages to raise money for the poor and the needy. He once said, '*I* feel wonderful – it's my *body* that's dying'. A young French lady I met in Italy years ago, a lady whose parents had died at Auschwitz, told me that she had forgiven the Nazis. Her European travels were part of a personal campaign to take her story to the media. She had a story to tell, a story about hatred and genocide – and a story about forgiveness.

These are some striking examples of styled creative responses to stress. Each individual has gone beyond the limited confines of typical (and typically negative) responses to stress. They reveal resilience, patience and forgiveness. Such people are numerous, and we can all learn from their example to redirect our powerful emotions towards constructive ends.

t w o

sources of stress

where stress comes from

What makes stress management difficult is that, as I explained with the HERO principle, sources of stress are all around us (that is, our reactions to all kinds of outside influences are potentially stressful). Our jobs, our children, our daily traffic jams, our personal relationships and our financial situation all require us to respond, and typically we do this in very unhelpful, unhealthy ways. In short, we are reacting all the time to both internal and external stresses, and yet our feelings are entirely within our control.

We can divide stressors into two categories: predictable and unpredictable. The first category includes those events that affect our lives over a period of time. For example, a couple gradually learns to adjust to each other's character and idiosyncrasies. This adjustment is usually a slow process. But the knowledge that each gains of the other over time can make each personality seem somewhat more predictable. The birth of a child is another predictable stressor as one of life's natural stages. The woman goes through a well-recognized process of physiological and psychological changes that accompany pregnancy and birth. The father, meanwhile, learns to adjust to the needs of the mother and the new family member.

On the other hand, some of life's more serious stressors arrive entirely unpredictably, or we simply may fail to predict them. For example, the couple may discover unpleasant truths about each other's personalities and hidden expectations soon after they have started the relationship. Or they may not fully realize the sacrifices that a new child requires until they have experienced many sleepless nights. A lack of preparedness or understanding can aggravate those stressors that might otherwise be quite manageable.

predictable stressors

Let's look at two of life's major predictable stressors, namely, work and unrealistic expectations.

Work

Many people dislike their jobs. They go to work because they have to earn a living. But job dissatisfaction increases your daily level of stress. Try assessing your own level of job satisfaction by answering the Job Satisfaction Survey (below).

Job Satisfaction Survey

Circle the number of each item according to how well it describes your typical feelings or behaviour at work. The numbers represent a spectrum between the low-satisfaction comment on the left and the high-satisfaction comment on the right. Do not think too much about each one because you may describe what is ideal rather than customary for you.

1. I seldom feel satisfied with my job.	1 2 3 4 5 6 7 8 9 10	I often feel satisfied with my job.
2. I seldom feel I make enough money for what I do.	1 2 3 4 5 6 7 8 9 10	I often feel I make enough money for what I do.

3. I seldom feel I have a chance for doing better.

1 2 3 4 5 6 7 8 9 10

I often feel I have a chance for doing better.

4. I seldom get along with my colleagues.

1 2 3 4 5 6 7 8 9 10

I often get along with my colleagues.

5. I seldom feel part of the work team.

1 2 3 4 5 6 7 8 9 10

I often feel part of the work team.

6. I often feel over-loaded with work.

1 2 3 4 5 6 7 8 9 10

I seldom feel over-loaded with work.

7. I seldom have time for my family.

1 2 3 4 5 6 7 8 9 10

I often have time for my family.

8. I seldom have enthusiasm for my job.

1 2 3 4 5 6 7 8 9 10

I often have enthusi-asm for my job.

9. I seldom find my job challenging.

1 2 3 4 5 6 7 8 9 10

I often find my job challenging.

10. I seldom trust others' intentions.

1 2 3 4 5 6 7 8 9 10

I often trust others' intentions.

11. I seldom feel sup-ported for my ideas.

1 2 3 4 5 6 7 8 9 10

I often feel supported for my ideas.

12. I often feel an urge to get out of my present job.

1 2 3 4 5 6 7 8 9 10

I seldom feel an urge to get out of my present job.

13. I seldom set realis-tic and challenging goals.

1 2 3 4 5 6 7 8 9 10

I often set realistic and challenging goals.

14. I seldom meet my deadlines.

1 2 3 4 5 6 7 8 9 10

I often meet my dead-lines.

15. I seldom feel my job makes a differ-ence.

1 2 3 4 5 6 7 8 9 10

I often feel my job makes a difference.

16. I seldom feel appreciated by my supervisor.

1 2 3 4 5 6 7 8 9 10

I often feel appreci- ated by my supervisor.

17. I work for the money.

1 2 3 4 5 6 7 8 9 10

I work for the joy of it.

18. I often compare my performance with that of others.

1 2 3 4 5 6 7 8 9 10

I seldom compare my performance with that of others.

19. I seldom take ade- quate time for lunch and breaks.

1 2 3 4 5 6 7 8 9 10

I often take adequate time for lunch and breaks.

20. I seldom feel capable of handling conflict.

1 2 3 4 5 6 7 8 9 10

I often feel capable of handling conflict.

21. I often have per- sonality clashes with my supervisor.

1 2 3 4 5 6 7 8 9 10

I seldom have person- ality clashes with my supervisor.

22. I often feel bored at work.

1 2 3 4 5 6 7 8 9 10

I seldom feel bored at work.

23. I often feel stress from noise pollution or poor working con- ditions.

1 2 3 4 5 6 7 8 9 10

I seldom feel stress from noise pollution or poor working con- ditions.

24. I have difficulty handling criticism of my work.

1 2 3 4 5 6 7 8 9 10

I can handle criticism of my work.

25. I seldom feel satis- fied with my own per- formance.

1 2 3 4 5 6 7 8 9 10

I often feel satisfied with my own perfor- mance.

26. I seldom stand up for my rights.

1 2 3 4 5 6 7 8 9 10

I often stand up for my rights.

27. I often have to take work home.

1 2 3 4 5 6 7 8 9 10

I seldom have to take work home.

28. I seldom feel my talents are used.

1 2 3 4 5 6 7 8 9 10

I often feel my talents are used.

29. I often have to put up with too much bureaucracy.

1 2 3 4 5 6 7 8 9 10

I seldom have to put up with bureaucracy.

30. I often feel I am discriminated against.

1 2 3 4 5 6 7 8 9 10

I seldom feel I am discriminated against.

Please remember that the purpose of the survey is to make you aware of the level of stress at your work. Whether you get a high or a low score is not important. However if you need some kind of feedback, you can connect the circles with a pencil to get a zigzag line. Then turn the book on its side to see a line that goes up and down between the positive and negative sides of the spectrum. Now go back and read the items once more. Think about each situation and your typical response. Whenever stress becomes excessive, there are three possible strategies to follow:

1. Avoid the situation.
2. Change the situation.
3. Cope with the situation by changing your behaviour.

For example, if you feel stressed because you do too much overtime work, you can:

1. Change your job.
2. Ask for less overtime work.
3. Manage your time more efficiently, setting new priorities.
4. Learn new skills.

If you find your level of job satisfaction is generally low, you could try to make your work more rewarding (whether you work in or out of the home). Consider the following suggestions:

1. Use reward and punishment. When you finish your daily task, reward yourself. Indulge yourself with a small gift or your favourite dessert, or just a simple and honest pat on the back. On the other hand, if you have not managed your share of the work, stay and finish it. But try not to take your work home, and don't take your problems home with you either. Be like Agent 007, James Bond, who, on reaching the safety of a ship after being chased by a shark, removed his black diving suit to reveal a formal white dinner suit beneath. He introduced himself with his usual smile and 'My name is Bond, James Bond'. No mention of the cold water or the hungry shark! So before entering your home, take off your dark 'work' suit and dress your thoughts for pleasure.

2. Do the hardest task first. Don't leave the toughest task for the end of the day when you are tired. Organize your day and tackle the most difficult thing first. When your energy level is higher, the hard things don't seem so difficult.

3. Offer constructive criticism and welcome it from others. After reading about your job, you will have ideas for improvement. Don't insist that your ideas be implemented (thereby causing more stress). If you are a boss, be open to your employees' ideas and suggestions. Remember that a mind is like a parachute: it works only when it opens.

4. Be your own interior designer. Make regular changes at your workplace. Hang a new poster on the wall, bring in a new coffee mug or set of picture frames. Make these changes as often as you need to. Variety is the spice of life, and an attractive and friendly workplace makes you feel more positive about what you do and where you do it.

However, if all else fails, consider leaving your job for a more appropriate one. Consult a job counsellor for guidance, and then make a decision.

Let me end with the advice the great Leonardo da Vinci gave about work: 'Every now and then, go away, take a little relaxation, because when you come back to your work your judgement will be surer. To remain constantly at your work will cause you to lose power of judgement. Go some distance away, because then the work appears smaller and more of it can be taken in at a glance, and a lack of harmony or proportion is more readily seen.' Although Leonardo's advice was given in regard to painting and sculpture, it can be applied to all kinds of activities.

Unrealistic Goals and Expectations

The setting of goals has many benefits. Having a goal gives direction and purpose to our lives. Moreover, goals allow us to accomplish more (see 'Goal-Setting' in Chapter 8 below). But statistics show that first-year university students have the highest rate of suicide in their age group. Why? A new environment? A stressful new lifestyle? Possibly. The most important factor in the high rate of first-year suicides, however, is their parents' unrealistic expectations.

So don't embrace the impossible. Aim for achievable goals, and take your ambitions one step at a time. That way, you will minimize your stress level while maximizing your potential for long-term achievement.

unpredictable stressors

Major life changes are stressors that present greater challenges than everyday problems. Keep in mind that it is not only negative changes that are stressful. The experience of falling in love may be as stressful as the ending of a relationship. Similarly, the challenges of a new job, a new home, and a new neighbourhood are among life's most testing, even though many aspects of such changes – meeting new people, taking on new responsibilities and discovering new leisure opportunities – can be exciting too. In this section, however, we will consider some of the traumatic changes that can occur unexpectedly, and which require us to tap into all our internal and external resources in order to cope successfully.

Death of a Loved One

Though many refuse to accept it, death is a natural event. Sooner or later we all die, yet most of us avoid thinking about it. We hear this evasiveness in our language: we talk of 'passing on', 'resting at peace', or 'meeting our maker', not 'dying'. Though we can rationalize the idea of death, few of us can accept death wholeheartedly as an inevitable stage of life. Most of us only realize the necessity of this acceptance when suddenly, unexpectedly, a loved one or someone close to us dies. Then we are faced with a severe challenge.

I remember vividly the day I received a phone call from Iran and my uncle gave me the news of my grandmother's death. At that time I was living in Italy and couldn't go to the funeral. Achingly depressed, I cried for several days. I would picture my grandmother in my imagination and then be suddenly shaken anew by the realization that I would never see her again. I also felt guilty for not adequately reciprocating the love and sacrificial care she gave to our family.

Fortunately, I had a loving group of friends and relatives around me. They were my support team. Their willing ears and soft shoulders helped me in my grief – even if most of the time they only listened.

Another death that affected me enormously was the death of my father. After seven years of suffering resulting from a car accident, he died. Although for the last two years his health had deteriorated dramatically, the news was still a shock. A few months before his death he suffered an infarct. The doctors told us that his body was so fragile that performing CPR in the case of an emergency would have broken his ribs and done him more harm. They advised the family to give them written permission not to resuscitate my father in the case of an emergency and allow him to die. The family discussed it and agreed with the doctors' advice.

When he was ill, I never thought that my father's death would create such an empty space in my life. I thought that I would be used to it, since he was bedridden for the last year of his life and could not speak any more. All he could do was to acknowledge my presence with a smile or a nod. I did not realize that I would miss him so much. It was only after his death that I realized how much of a powerful presence he had had. Although his body and mind had been dying, his spirit had affected me powerfully during my visits. How else could I explain that empty feeling after his death?

For the first few weeks after my father's death I dreamt about him every night. Some of the dreams were serene and others were disturbing nightmares. Gradually, over a period of three or four months, the dreams became less frequent. It seems that my subconscious mind needed that time to sort out many unfinished things.

Life is a never-ending journey of growth and development, and dying does not necessarily mean the end of life. This belief helped me accept the death of my father. I kept reminding myself that he would be closer to me now than when he was fragile and bedridden. His spirit was now free from the limitations of a weakened body and mind. He did not stop being my father when he died: he is still my father and I am still his son. Our father-son relationship continues at a more elevated level.

The feelings that accompany grief – shock, denial, anger, guilt, depression – are natural and inevitable. But it's our *responses* to this experience that make the difference and can transform the meaning of the most tragic event. As Erik Blumenthal writes in *To Understand and Be Understood*,

> We are all decision-making human beings who decide on some level to do everything we do. Each thought, each feeling, each desire, each expectation and each expression is the result of a decision, for the most part made subconsciously. (p. 10)

We are in charge of our emotions and behaviour. We may not be able to prevent the death of a person we love, but we can choose how to respond to it. We can respond by destructive behaviour, such as incessant crying, refusing to eat or care for our health, behaving violently towards others or ourselves, or abusing drugs and alcohol. Or, we can respond more creatively and spiritually. If we have religious belief we can be steadied by our faith in the Creator and the progress of the soul after death. We can pray, talk about and express our emotions creatively, accept death as 'a messenger of joy', and view our grief as a test for our spiritual growth.

Helping a Bereaved Person

We have already touched on the emotions that accompany bereavement. The first and most common of these is denial. 'Not me, not this, not now' are the words that race through our minds at the first hearing of tragic news; 'it can't be true; they've made a mistake'. People experience this feeling in different degrees. One person may deny the death of their loved one for a few days; another might hire a medium to try to communicate with the person. Some people quickly learn to let go of the past, others dwell upon it. The shock of bereavement affects people in different ways; it may, on first impact, even precipitate a brief spasm of nervous, uncontrolled laughter.

During the first stage of their grieving, people may speak or act as though their loved one were still alive. You will need to be very patient with them at this time, and should refrain from insisting on acceptance of the fact that their loved one is gone. Listen to their grief, and console them as you can (see 'Tips for Good Listening', Chapter 7).

Soon their denial will give way to acceptance. But this acceptance also brings its own grief. The intensity of grief varies with the personal quality of their relationship with the deceased. You can encourage them to talk about and express their feelings. Listen without judging, and encourage them to talk about what they were able to give to and receive from that person. There is no point in dwelling on what they should have done or could have done.

Depression is always near at hand at the stage in the grieving process when the bereaved person realizes that the loved one is no longer with them and will never return. Some may feel guilty for not having given more. Listen to them with your heart. Despite your good intentions, don't try to console them with clichés, which might diminish or trivialize their feelings. To communicate your sympathy nonverbally, you might try a rapport exercise as outlined in Chapter 7. In order to change someone's emotional state, you need to join them in that state long enough to establish rapport. Then you can modify their emotional state by changing yours.

Keep in mind that helping a bereaved person cope with his or her grief can be very stressful, if not totally exhausting. Stay alert to your own physical and emotional health; don't neglect it. Find a balance between assisting the grieving process and keeping a healthy emotional distance from it. In this way the grief-stricken will not become too dependent on your care and attention. Do not hesitate to ask for help from a relative or friend or even a professional if you think you need support.

Traumatic Events

One day during my stay in Barcelona, a tragic news story flashed onto the television screen. A car bomb, evidently planted by a terrorist group, had exploded, badly injuring the wife and daughter of a member of the Spanish police force. The mother, Maria Jesus Gonzales, had lost an arm and a leg; her teenaged daughter Irene had lost both legs. The TV screen was filled with pictures of the blast's first aftershocks. The young girl, disoriented and not yet aware of what had happened to her, tried to stand up. I felt enraged and helpless. I had to do something.

A few weeks later I went to Madrid to visit the woman and her daughter in hospital. I took a Native Canadian ('Buffalo Bill') hat for the young girl and a prayer book for her mother. When I introduced myself, the mother greeted me with a broad smile; I was utterly surprised to see such serenity on her face. We went to the cafeteria to chat.

I was longing to know the source of her composure and apparent contentment. She mentioned three things as being most important. One was her faith in God. Everything happens with a reason, she said; her faith had helped her to accept her sufferings with patience. Strangely, unexpectedly, I found she also had a positive attitude towards the tragic incident. She busied her thoughts with what she could do with her body now, rather than what she could have done had she still had her missing limbs. Her third resource was the support of her family, friends and strangers. They all showered her and her daughter with unconditional love. They were both supported by a nurturing environment that encouraged them to share their feelings.

I became interested in interviewing other Spanish terrorist victims. Six years earlier, in one of the worst terrorist actions in Spain's history, a bomb had gone off in a supermarket in Barcelona. Many were killed, including a woman and her two daughters.

I met the father of that family, Alvaro Cabrerizo. Once more, I wondered how he had coped with the death of his wife and daughters. He told me that at first he hadn't wanted to believe in their deaths, and that he had refused to accept the truth for several months. During that time he drank heavily and cried all day. He felt angry at the world and guilty for not having been with his wife and daughters in the supermarket. He even refused the help and support of his friends and relatives.

But his friends didn't give up. They continued to offer their support until he was able to accept it. Gradually, he acknowledged his emotions and dealt with them. He consulted a psychologist who helped him express his anger and guilt creatively. Eventually he began to resume responsibility for his feelings and his health, regained his willingness to work, and set goals for the future. He told me his primary resources were three: faith in God, a loving group of supportive people, and a willingness to live on.

My interviewees seemed to share many of the spiritual responses to crises that Dr Abdu'l-Missagh Ghadirian mentions in his book *Ageing*:

- greater reliance on personal faith and beliefs
- greater capacity to accept pain and suffering
- awareness of one's own helplessness and imperfection
- acknowledgement of a supreme source of might and
   perfection: the Creator
- reliance on prayers and meditation
- a heightened sense of purpose in life. (p. 75)

Accidents are unpredictable. They happen without warning. We can learn from the example of a mother and her teenaged daughter who deal with their tragedy by focusing on the future rather than dwelling on the past. Or the case of a father whose entire family is randomly, senselessly destroyed, but who mobilizes his resources and looks to the future with optimism. We too can focus our thoughts and energies on strengthening our character and developing our inner resources. We too can console ourselves with the knowledge that the power of the human spirit is greater than the most painful and tragic event.

Natural Disasters

While we may sometimes blame accidents on human beings, we blame natural disasters on the actions of Nature. Nevertheless, feelings of helplessness at the hands of such forces can certainly overwhelm us.

When my parents moved to a small village in Iran called Abhar as Bahá'í pioneers in the 1940s, they endured a host of hardships. As well as the predictable persecution and discrimination, Nature added its own troubles. One of the most serious of hardships was caused by a river that ran through the middle of the village. This capricious water-way was known as 'Dalee Chay', the crazy river. Every now and then it would flood the village.

The second flood, my mother told me, was the worst. The day was cloudy; soon a heavy storm gathered, and the rain began to fall steadily. The river's water level rose rapidly, and it flooded the streets of the village. Soon the water began to fill the house, so my father took every-one up to the flat roof, where they watched as the rising flood waters took over the village. The rain was so heavy that one of my brothers, then three years old, said 'God has opened up all the taps', and every-one laughed.

Gradually all the rooms in the house were flooded. My family saw their belongings float away in the muddy water. As the walls began to collapse under the weight of the water, terrible danger loomed. Four metre waves swept away whole households. My parents prayed to God for protection amidst the chaos and destruction.

Suddenly, the surging flood waters caused the collapse of a house further up the street, and the direction of the water flow changed; our family was miraculously saved. They waited for the rain to ease and the flood level to subside. That horrible day was 3 November 1957.

After this event, a serenity came over my family: belief in God, patience and a sense of humour had lent them a spiritual defence in the face of a horrendously unpredictable situation.

Losing Your Job

The 1990s have been an exciting time so far. Technological accomplishments in the fields of robotics, communication and information processing have set the stage for an increasingly competitive business market. Perhaps one can sum up the spirit of this decade in two words: constant change. Sudden and unpredictable changes in the political, social and economic arenas have affected the business world. Organizations have difficulty in keeping up with these changes. Up until a few decades ago large Japanese companies were setting long-term goals, forecasting the market trends 200 years in advance! Now even a forecast for the next 20 years will be unrealistic.

In the 1960s, people were dissatisfied and disillusioned by large organizations, mainly because they could not meet the needs of their employees. In the 1970s, there were major improvements in safely procedures, company policies, fringe benefits and the treatment of women and ethnic minorities. These improvements, with increasing concern for the human element, continued in the 1980s with higher budgets allocated to staff training and development. However, in the late 1990s, many companies have made major cuts in the number of employees. An increasing number of large organizations have shown a preference for hiring part-time staff, who do not enjoy the same benefits as full-time employees, and are therefore cheaper. This tendency has led to an unstable labour market. It seems that we can no longer expect to be employed by the same company for a long time.

Losing your job can be a devastating experience. The financial loss may not be as important as its emotional and mental aspects. Many people feel that they have failed, losing their self-esteem and blaming themselves or others for losing their job. Often religious people feel that God has abandoned them.

In some cases, losing your job can be a rewarding experience if you view it as a turning point. You can take some time to re-evaluate your goals and consider other careers – or perhaps the time is right to start your own business. Maybe you need to upgrade your skills and knowledge. Visiting a career counsellor can be a valuable move. This can be an exciting time if you keep yourself motivated about learning new things.

Here are some tips to help you go through the stressful time between jobs:

- Remind yourself that you are a worthwhile and capable person. You do not lose your skills and experience – you carry them with you. This period of stress will help you tap into your inner resources and potential.

- Every morning, get dressed and get out of the house. Plan your week as if you are working. Don't fall into the trap of getting up late and walking around in your dressing gown and slippers just because you don't have to go anywhere. Staying at home lounging around makes you feel depressed.

- Remember to have fun. Do not think that you don't deserve to enjoy yourself because you are not working. Include visits to the cinema and museums, or alternative and inexpensive activities, in your weekly plan.

- Do some thinking about what you want to do next. Do you want to find a job in the same field as before? Or do you want to change your career altogether? Do you want to start your own business? Talk to a job counsellor and make a decision. Then make a plan of action and get to work. Remember that 70% of available positions may not be advertised. Select the companies that you want to work for and write speculative letters.

Financial Difficulties

Virtually everyone has experienced financial problems at some time in their life. It seems that it is a universal law that we must go through economic ups and downs in one way or another. Unemployment figures have risen in the last few years. More and more people are losing their jobs, which often results in financial difficulties. The best strategy to follow is careful management of your earnings and savings during the prosperous times, so that if the worst should happen and you lose your job, you will have something to fall back on when times become lean.

There is a financial law that sounds ridiculously simple, but is very often overlooked: always spend less than you earn. There are a number of inventions that lure people into breaking this fundamental law. Credit cards, for example, are practical tools in everybody's hands. They are useful in case you run out of cash, but their disadvantage is that they are so easy to use. Another problem is the apparent attractiveness of payment systems available for shoppers. Advertisers repeatedly remind us that it is possible to 'buy now and do not pay until next year!' This offer can be practical if it matches your well-planned budget. However, if you lack discipline and an effective personal money management system, such offers may cause you financial stress.

There are many resources available to help you plan a budget. You can benefit from consulting a financial advisor or reading books on money management. These resources help you set a realistic budget and track your spending on a regular basis. The most important thing is that you plan ahead to have enough financial security to be able to avoid the stressful times if you lose your job.

losing control

Unpredictable stressors have one thing in common: loss of control. One's fate seems out of one's hands. Life's most stressful and demanding challenges all seem to have this key ingredient. It appears that we all have a need to feel in control of our lives to some extent. A study of a group of police officers that asked them to rate a list of stressors revealed that they thought negative press coverage was more stressful than making a dangerous arrest. Why? During an arrest they felt that they were still in control. But the press's portrayal of their work was beyond their control.

A classic experiment with rats showed the relationship between control and physical health. The experimenters administered mild shocks to two laboratory rats. The shocks were strong enough to irritate, but not strong enough to harm. Only one rat had the opportunity to prevent the shock by turning a wheel. All shocks were preceded by a warning signal. Whenever the first rat failed to turn the wheel, both rats received the same shock. The results revealed that the second rat was more prone to ulcers. The difference in their health was telling: one had a measure of control over what was happening to him, one had none.

What can we do when the situation is beyond our control? Sometimes we may feel like rats in a cage, but in reality we have spiritual and mental resources that allow us to be much more creative in the face of stress. We must avoid getting trapped by the fight-or-flight response. By transcending the limited and fixed pattern of our behaviour we are able to live through the most stressful times with endurance, dignity and a sense of humour. Helping you to learn and practise such skills is the goal of this book.

PART

two

four dimensions of stress management

three

the spiritual dimension

M any scientists (and other people) are rediscovering the classical idea that spirit is connected to mind and body. They have come to the conclusion that neglecting any aspect of our nature impairs the rest of it. This holistic approach emphasizes the importance of the human body as well as our emotions and thoughts. More and more physicians are taking into account aspects of their patients' condition other than their physical symptoms. The skilled physician takes the most complete view possible.

The holistic theory applies to stress management too. In order to regain your balance in life, you need to pay attention to all of these dimensions: spiritual, mental, emotional and physical.

For most people the word 'spiritual' is synonymous with the word 'religion'. But spirituality is not religiosity. Spirituality is our life-long goal. From birth until death, we strive to develop our character and our conduct. A spiritual person is one who strives to acquire human virtues.

In coping with the stress and suffering life inevitably brings, the spiritual dimension is the most important of all. No matter how much deep breathing you practise in times of stress, without a spiritual approach to life you will have difficulty in coping. The following pages present some of the spiritual resources available to you.

prayer or contemplation

For many people, praying is an effective way of coping with stress and suffering. Their belief in God's love and justice helps them to be patient. Prayers help them to persevere through calamities and to endure hardships. When they pray, they admit their powerlessness and God's might and power. This humility gives them strength and courage.

Those with no particular religious faith but who have a sense of their own spirituality may use contemplation instead of prayer – an inner quietness similar to meditation (see page 45).

Moreover, praying or contemplation is good for you. Numerous studies have indicated the beneficial power of prayer on the body. People who pray have a lower incidence of hypertension and stroke, for instance, while praying helps to transform worry into serenity.

Here are five steps Shoghi Effendi, the Guardian of the Bahá'í Faith, once suggested for the use of prayer as a means of solving problems:

5 Steps to Effective Prayer

Step 1 Pray and meditate about the problem or concern. Use the prayers of the Manifestations of God (that is, the traditional Christian, Jewish, Muslim, Buddhist and Bahá'í prophets) as they have greater power than prayers you may fashion yourself. Then remain in the silence of contemplation for a few minutes.

Step 2 Arrive at a decision and hold to it. This decision is usually born during contemplation. It may seem almost impossible to accomplish, but if it seems to be the answer to a prayer or a way of solving the problem, then immediately take the next step.

Step 3 Have the determination to carry the decision through. Many fail here. The decision, budding into determination, fades instead into a vague wish or longing. When determination is born, immediately take the next step.

Step 4   Have faith and confidence that the power will flow through you, the door will open, and the right thought, message, principle or book will be given to you. Have confidence, and the right thing will come to your need. Then as you rise from prayer, take at once the fifth step.

Step 5   Act as though your prayer has been answered. Then move with tireless, ceaseless energy towards achieving your solution. And as you act, you, yourself, will become a magnet, attracting more power to you, until you become an unobstructed channel for the divine power to flow through you.

Many pray but do not remain for the last half of the first step, a few moments of silent contemplation. Some who meditate arrive at a decision but fail to hold to it. Then again, many lack the determination to carry the decision through, and still fewer have the confidence that the right thing will come to their need. But how many remember to act as though their prayers have been answered? As it says in Bahá'í holy writings: 'Greater than the prayer is the spirit in which it is uttered. And greater than the way it is uttered is the spirit in which it is carried out.'

meditation

Don't be puzzled or intimidated by the word 'meditation'. Meditation simply means quietening your mind. To meditate, you don't have to wear orange clothes, change your religion or adopt impossible body positions. Meditation is a state of mind.

Through your brain, meditation has a beneficial effect on your body. The language of the brain is electrical – electro-encephalograms record voltage changes in the brain. When you meditate, you enter a relaxed state and your brain produces Alpha waves at eight to thirteen cycles per second. (In contrast, during active, normal, outward wakefulness your brain produces Beta waves at some fourteen to fifty cycles per second.) The Alpha rhythm is characteristic of an alert wakefulness.

When you meditate or use visual imagery for relaxation, you stimulate the right side of the brain, the part responsible for passiveness, inward awareness, floating sensations, and feelings of calm and serenity.

Set aside thirty minutes a day to practise meditating. If you think you will get bored sitting for thirty minutes by yourself, begin with ten minutes. Then, as you practise, increase the length of time. There is no standard time for meditating. Indian gurus and Buddhist monks meditate some eight hours a day. I suggest that you meditate for at least twenty minutes in order to begin to make yourself fully comfortable with the experiences it induces.

4 Steps to Effective Meditation

Step 1 Sit in a quiet place. Wear loose, comfortable clothing and choose a position that suits you. Make sure you will not be disturbed for at least twenty minutes.

Step 2 Close your eyes. Breathe deeply and evenly through your nose. Guide your breathing for thirty seconds or so, then let your subconscious take control and continue with deep and even breathing. Scan your body for areas of tension. Begin at your feet and progress up to your head. Focus your attention on each part of your body and let go of all tension.

Step 3 As you breathe deeply, say to yourself words like 'calm', 'quiet', and 'serene' – words that help you relax. Become aware of your breathing once again to maintain its peaceful, steady pace. If your breathing is not deep and even, breathe in and out very deeply ten times. Then let the air breathe you.

Step 4 Let your mind wander. Let thoughts come and go; be passive. You can also direct your thoughts toward a single specific thing (such as the words you are repeating to yourself), or you can focus on specific parts of your body in order to deepen the feeling of relaxation.

The key to meditation is a passive attitude. Let your thoughts go where they will as your body eases you into a feeling of comfort. The more you 'try' to relax, or the more you force yourself to meditate, the less you will accomplish. Don't expect to discover your 'third eye' or fore-tell future events after thirty minutes of meditating. And don't worry about doing it perfectly. Whatever way you do it is right for you. Many get frustrated because they don't get results right away, but the secret of successful meditation is the will to accept and encourage the waves of relaxation and passive thought as each takes control of your body.

Practise regularly in order to notice the benefits of meditation. Oxygen consumption is reduced, for instance, while galvanic skin resis-tance increases, a sign that the blood flow is even throughout your body. Moreover, you gain confidence in your ability to calm your body and mind, so regular meditation helps you feel serene and prepared to face the challenges of your daily life.

forgiveness

Two monks were out walking at daybreak one rainy day, when they came to a place where the road was submerged in two feet of water. A young woman in a silk dress happened by, terrified of the muddy road. One of the monks guessed that she wanted to cross, and without hesita-tion picked the young woman up and carried her to the other side of the road. As the two monks returned to the monastery, they did not speak. But when they got to the monastery, the second monk exploded: 'You are a disgrace to the whole order. You know that we are not even allowed to speak to a woman, let alone carry one in our arms.' The first monk replied calmly, 'I put her down on the other side of the road. Are you still carrying her?'

Of all of the virtues we need to acquire, forgiveness is the most impor-tant one for stress management. The ability to give up past resentments is crucial to your health and spiritual growth. Holding on to grievances fuels the fires of resentment and stress.

Have you ever tried to reconcile two people in a conflict while each maintained that he or she would 'never forgive' the other? No matter how you try to persuade people in this frame of mind to set aside the past, they resist and refuse to forgive. But my question to such people would be this: If you don't forgive and let go of past resentments, who is going to suffer? You or the other person? By failing to forgive, we become the target of our own bitterness. Resentment clutters our soul with unpleasant feelings that rob us of energy without our knowing it. We become the victim of our own stress-induced decisions. This state of artificially raised adrenaline can then give rise to a series of health problems ranging from migraine headaches to ulcers.

Consider the following mystical Persian story:

A wanderer trudged along a seemingly endless road. He was loaded down with all sorts of burdens. A heavy sack of sand hung on his back; a thick water bag was slung across his body. In his right hand he carried an oddly shaped stone, in his left, a boulder. Around his neck an old millstone dangled from a frayed rope. Rusty chains, with which he dragged heavy weights through the dusty sand, cut into his ankles. On his head the man was balancing a half-rotten pumpkin. With every step he took, the chains rattled.

Moaning and groaning, he moved forward step by step, complaining of his hard fate and the weariness that tormented him. On the way a farmer met him in the searing heat of midday and asked him, 'Oh tired wanderer, why do you load yourself down with this stone and this boulder?'

'It's awfully stupid', replied the wanderer, 'but I hadn't noticed them before'. With that, he threw the rocks away and felt much lighter.

After going a long way farther down the road, the wanderer was met by another farmer, who asked, 'Tell me, tired wanderer, why do you trouble yourself with the half-rotten pumpkin on your head, and why do you drag those heavy weights behind you on chains?'

The wanderer answered, 'I'm very glad you pointed that out to me. I didn't realize what I was doing to myself.' He took off the chains and tossed the pumpkin into a ditch alongside the road. Again, he felt lighter. But the farther he went, the more he began to suffer again.

A third farmer coming from a field watched the wanderer with amazement and said, 'Oh, good man, you are carrying sand in that sack, but what you see far off in the distance is more sand than you could ever carry. And your big water bag – it looks as if you plan to cross the Kavir Desert. All the while there's a clear stream flowing alongside you, which will accompany you on your way for a long time.'

Upon hearing this, the wanderer tore open the water bag and emptied its brackish water onto the path. Then he filled a hole with the sand from his knapsack.

He stood there passively and looked into the sinking sun. The last rays sent their light to him. He glanced down at himself, saw the heavy millstone around his neck and suddenly realized that it was the stone that was causing him to walk so bent over. He untied the rope and threw the millstone as far as he could into the river. Freed from his burdens, he wandered on through the cool of the evening to find lodging.

Are you carrying a sack of sand, an old millstone, rusty chains or a half-rotten pumpkin? Isn't it time to throw them away? Is there anyone in your life you have not forgiven? I invite you to let go of the past. Even if they don't forgive you, *you* can do your part.

I am well aware that this task is not easy. But even if you were to go as far as contacting someone to offer forgiveness, your eventual liberation from these negative influences is worth all the mixed feelings you may experience. Empty your heart of hatred and allow love to take its place. Forgiveness is a sign of grandeur.

There are several ways you can help yourself forgive someone. If the person in question is no longer living, or you do not wish to confront him or her, use the chair technique. Imagine this person is sitting in front of you or beside you in a chair. Talk to him or her. Express your feelings. Be uninhibited. Say whatever comes into your head. Then let go of your resentment and feel forgiveness instead. You may even want to hug the person or shake hands. If talking to an empty chair strikes you as a bit strange, write them a letter. In that letter write whatever comes to your mind. Let your thoughts roam. Express all your relevant feelings. Then, at the end, forgive him or her.

I know many people who at the very mention of someone they hate become furious and begin to relive some ugly or unfortunate incident. They have not let go of the past. Let go of yours, and watch your life improve.

faith

Each of us acts in accordance with what we believe to be 'true' or 'possible'. Most of our behaviour, in fact, is the result of our faith or belief system. One experiment that illustrates the magnitude of the power of belief was conducted by Dr Henry Beecher of the Harvard Medical School. He told a group of patients suffering from post-operative pain that he was giving them morphine. In fact only half the group got real morphine; the other half got the placebo – sugar pills. The researchers wanted to know if the group receiving the placebo would feel any less pain, that is, whether *thinking* that they had taken a painkiller would influence their reaction to their discomfort. The results were astonishing. The researchers discovered that the placebo was 77% as effective as the real morphine!

This experiment demonstrates the power of belief over the functioning of the human body. In our culture morphine is the most potent drug used to relieve pain. Patients in the placebo group experienced relief merely by *expecting* that the supposed morphine would ease their suffering. Our beliefs rule our lives.

Similarly, our expectations about people and events have powerful implications for our daily life. Not too long ago, while I was working on this book, I witnessed how faith can work miracles. Late one afternoon a gentleman in his late seventies was struck by a car while he was crossing the street. When his doctors realized that his condition was critical, they ordered him to be transferred to a bigger hospital in Toronto. From the beginning the doctors had warned the family that the man was very badly injured and probably would not live long. We rejected the doctors' opinion; we had a right to do so; the patient was our father.

That night, after a series of emergency operations, he was sent to the intensive care unit, where patients whose lives are threatened are cared for continuously. When my brother and I entered that room full of strange machines and hoses and hook-ups, my father was conscious, but barely recognizable. His face was swollen, and a metallic tube ran from an odd-looking contraption into the top of his head. I was told that its function was to prevent or reduce pressure on the brain.

I softly approached my father and took his right hand. Then I whispered in his ear in a deliberate and loving tone: 'Dear Dad. It's me, Arthur, your son. You've got to fight. Fight! We are with you.' Then I asked him to squeeze my hand if he had heard me. He did.

Gradually over the following year my father's condition improved. Soon he could recognize his sons and daughters, and he regained his speech. He still couldn't move his legs, however, since both of them had been broken in several places. Also, one of his knees had been badly broken and he couldn't straighten it out. His doctor told us that we had better get our father accustomed to a wheelchair. She predicted that he would never walk again. Once again, we rejected her opinion.

My brother David slowly and persistently planted the idea in my father's brain that one day he would walk again. At first my father didn't pay any attention. After all, he had what he thought was firm evidence that walking was extremely unlikely: there was the opinion of the doctor, the excruciating pain in his right knee when he tried to straighten it, and the advice of his friends and relatives that he should begin to cope with what looked like the inevitable consequences of the accident.

But my brother continued to insist that he could walk. Soon my brother's contagious faith began to change my father's outlook. He began co-operating with his physiotherapists. His desire to walk became stronger every day. When his therapists asked him to do one more exercise, he would do two or three. And each day he was anxious to get on to his exercises. It seemed that nothing could stop him.

His condition improved. Then one day we received a call from the hospital that he had fallen from his wheelchair and suffered a minor injury. When we went to his room we found him with a black eye. He had tried to stand up but couldn't straighten out his right leg. He had lost his balance and fallen against his bed, hitting his head on the corner of it. We urged him to have patience, to remember that he would heal gradually, not all of a sudden. One week later another call from the hospital told us of yet another fall. We got used to seeing him with cuts and bruises on his face and hands.

Five months passed. One day we walked into his hospital room to find him gone from his bed. We saw someone standing in the washroom washing his hands. We couldn't believe our eyes! It was our father! Some weeks later he began to walk with the aid of a walking frame and then finally all by himself. A few months later he was able to go for his daily walk without any kind of assistance whatsoever.

What made my father walk? What mechanism or resource did he use to break through his physical limitation? How do we explain his miraculous recovery? His doctor would probably classify his case as a 'spontaneous recovery'. But it's probably more accurate to consider his healing a triumph of faith over experience.

Hypnotic phenomena offer other examples of the power of faith. In my training as a hypnotherapist, I have learned the amazing effects of suggestion on the body. In one of my early training sessions, I was the guinea pig for a demonstration on local anaesthesia. Through suggestion, the demonstrator relaxed me, then assured me that I would not feel any pain as a sterilized needle was stuck through the upper skin of my right hand. True to his prediction, there was no pain, because I believed in the trainer's abilities. He had proven his competence and won my confidence. I believed his suggestions and accepted them without doubt.

The history of hypnosis is filled with bewildering cases. Most dramatic of all are accounts of operations undertaken using hypnotic suggestion instead of anaesthesia. During such operations the hypnotherapist assists the patient in achieving a trance-like state sufficiently deep to control the pain.

In one such astonishing case, Dr Victor Rausch, a skilled hypnotherapist, used self-hypnosis to help him withstand the pain involved in undergoing the removal of his gall-bladder. His was an exceptional case because no anaesthesia or analgesic was used either during or after the operation. Dr Rausch, with whom I have since become acquainted, writes about his experience:

At the precise moment the incision was made, several things happened simultaneously. I felt a flowing sensation throughout my entire body . . . I was suddenly much more aware of my surroundings . . . My eyes were open and the operating team said that I had no visible tensing of the muscles, no change in my breathing, no flinching of my eyes and no change in facial expression.

Before the operation Dr Rausch had emphasized the importance of expectations:

I once more assured everyone [the operating team] that I felt fine, and tried to explain the importance of expectancy . . . I asked only that they mentally send me good 'vibes' and anticipate and expect total success.

Our understanding of the power of expectation is crucial to stress management. The person who takes drugs or drinks heavily during times of stress has a limited sense of his or her power to deal with the stress without such artificial or chemical help. Such people expect the drugs they take to calm their nerves, but they pay a very heavy – and unnecessary – price.

four

the mental dimension

Our minds can work for or against us. If we remain passive when we are under stress, we become victims of our own adrenalized states. But if we take charge of the situation, we can avoid many unpleasant symptoms. Consider the following ways of using your mind to your advantage.

visual imagery

Before writing this chapter, I went to the kitchen and took a big lemon out of the fridge. I cut it in half and squeezed its juice into my mouth. As I tasted the sour lemon juice . . . What is going on? Are you salivating? Why? There is no lemon juice in your mouth. But you still salivate! You have just witnessed one of the wonders of your mind: you respond to imaginary stimuli as if they were real.

By the way, did you know that Spain is one of the major producers of the world's lemons? Spain is a country blessed with a warm, sunny climate. In the summertime, Spanish beaches are the ideal place to relax. You can lie on white crystal sands, feel a gentle breeze caressing your body, and soak up the warmth of the sun while you listen to the whispering of gentle waves breaking on the shore. . . . If I continue with the image of the beach, very soon you begin to relax even if you are nowhere near a beach. The lesson to be learned from the examples of the lemon and the beach is this: you respond physiologically and psychologically to whatever images you hold in your mind.

You can use this principle to relax during your coffee break. Instead of artificially stimulating the release of adrenaline in your body by drinking coffee, you can go for a walk in a park, lie down on a beach, or go for a swim – all in your mind. Or you can use this technique before an interview. Instead of worrying about the interview, you can picture a time when you were relaxed and confident. Then picture your interview going well. Don't get bored or frustrated in waiting rooms or traffic hold-ups; use your imagination to take a trip in your mind.

Visual imagery is a powerful tool for healing. Many cancer patients use visualization techniques to try to accelerate their healing process. For example, some self-help programmes developed by the Canadian Cancer Society teach cancer patients to imagine that they have a light beam in their body that vaporizes cancer cells and strengthens the healthy ones. If you are interested in this subject, I can recommend to you Dr Bernie Siegel's wonderful book *Love, Medicine and Miracles*. In this book Dr Siegel explains how he helps his cancer patients use imagery to heal themselves. (I further explore healing imagery in Appendix I.)

I once taught a young man how to relieve his particular worry by using visual imagery. He had attended one of my seminars at the University of Waterloo and thought that I could help him. He said that whenever he wanted to pray or read the sacred writings of his religion, he 'saw' and 'felt' a monstrous, horribly sharp lance coming from behind to stab him in the back. This image prevented him from going near any prayer book or holy writings. He told me that he had formerly been sexually promiscuous and that he now wanted to fulfil one of his religious duties by praying, but that he could not bring himself to do so. I asked him if he had true faith in his religion. 'I asked for forgiveness and my faith is strong', he replied. I asked him to picture a shield becoming stronger as his faith grew day by day. I encouraged him to pay attention to the details of the shield's design, its colour, its size, and the smell and the feel of it. He responded by making his mental picture vividly detailed.

Once he had fully developed this powerful image, I asked him to wrap the shield around himself. Next I told him to imagine holding his prayer book and praying. Then I asked him to go ahead and do it. Timidly, he picked up the prayer book and began to smile. He said that he 'saw' the piercing lance trying to stab him. He said that he could even 'hear' the banging of the lance against the shield. One month later he told me that the lance didn't bother him any more.

Some people may find the technique of visual imagery difficult to master. If you are among those who think they cannot visualize, remember that all of us day-dream occasionally. And day-dreaming is a natural and instinctive way of using mental imagery. How often during a boring lecture have you found yourself thinking about your favourite hobby, and been far away from the lecture room in your imagination? You remain immersed in your 'movie' and are oblivious to your immediate surroundings until something snaps you to attention. This is an example of the kind of mental process I am describing. I have included later in this chapter a script you can use for relaxation through mental imagery (see 'A Peaceful Trip').

autogenic training

With visual imagery you relax your body by holding a picture in your mind, communicating with your body through mental images. With autogenic training you literally tell your body to relax. 'Autogenic' reactions are self-produced or self-generated ones. It's a form of training that was developed by Johannes Schultz and Wolfgang Luthe in Germany, and the basis for this technique of relaxation is a series of simple phrases that you repeat to yourself. Phrases such as 'my heart-beat is calm and regular' or 'my breathing is deep' have proved to be effective in producing the desired physiological changes in the body.

At first you may find it difficult to achieve autogenic reactions, but be patient and practise. As you practise, you will gain confidence. If you find that phrases like 'my breathing is deep and even' are not helping you, try different ones. Maybe putting the mental suggestion in the form of a question will help. For instance, you might say to yourself,

'I wonder how soon my breathing will become deep and even?' or you can say, 'I wonder which one of my hands will become warm first?'

5 Steps to Effective Autogenic Suggestion

Begin a relaxing session of autogenic suggestion by finding a comfortable and quiet place in which to lie down. Choose a time when you are unlikely to be disturbed.

Step 1 Loosen your clothing and remove your shoes.

Step 2 Sit somewhere comfortable, ideally in an armchair that supports your arms, your head and your legs.

Step 3 Put your arms at your sides without touching your body.

Step 4 Begin by mentally repeating each of the following phrases three to five times over, slowly and deliberately:

'My right hand is warm.'
'My left hand is warm.'
'My right arm is warm.'
'My left arm is warm.'
'Both my arms are warm.'
'My right foot is warm.'
'My left foot is warm.'
'My right leg is warm.'
'My left leg is warm.'
'Both my legs are warm.'
'My breathing is deep and comfortable.'
'My heartbeat is calm and regular.'
'My chest is relaxed.'
'My shoulder muscles are limp.'
'My neck muscles are limp.'
'My mouth is relaxed.'
'My tongue is relaxed.'
'My forehead is relaxed and cool.'
'My whole body is warm and refreshed.'

Step 5 When you open your eyes, stretch out your arms and legs. Slowly move your head and sit up.

Step 6 Remain seated for a few minutes before standing up. This allows you to reorient yourself and regain your alertness.

If you have never done relaxation exercises or meditation before, you'll be surprised at some changes in your body temperature. You will also experience some unfamiliar body sensations. These novel sensations include a feeling of dissociation from your body, and perhaps a tingling and twitching in your fingers. These sensations are quite natural.

Try an experiment. Measure your skin temperature during your sessions by taping a thermometer to one of your fingers. You'll notice that as your body becomes relaxed and your muscle tension decreases, your skin temperature increases. Experiment with this technique and enjoy the results.

self-talk

As you sit holding this book, you see black ink against the whiteness of the page. You can hear sounds around you and feel the temperature of your hands. There may be some objects in your peripheral vision. You feel the pressure where your body touches the chair. As you breathe in and out, you feel the texture of this page with your fingers. With each breath, you feel your chest falling and rising. Now you have an irresistible urge to swallow. Your mouth is watering. Have you swallowed your saliva yet?

Let me explain why I made you swallow (or at least made you salivate). Our mind has both conscious and subconscious functions, with the latter controlling a large number of activities in our bodies. Heart rate, saliva secretion, eye blinking, breathing, temperature changes, hormone secretion and many other bodily functions are controlled subconsciously. This is all work that is normally done automatically, without your being aware of it.

Until you finish reading this sentence, you are not aware of your right foot. Now that you have read the last two words of the last sentence, you have become aware of your right foot. Our consciousness of our bodies and of stimuli is limited. And thank goodness it is, because without a limited consciousness we would be overwhelmed by the amount of information we are constantly receiving. Imagine if you had consciously to control all the different muscles involved in walking. When you decide to walk, you don't have to think or say to yourself, 'Okay, now I bend this knee, put one foot forward, swing my arms', and so on. If you did, you wouldn't be able to get very far.

To see how complex the action of walking really is, observe a child just discovering how to walk. You will notice that walking has to be learned consciously. That is, the child has to learn through trial and error the correct sequence of muscle contraction and relaxation in all the muscles involved in this complicated, awkward process. The child tries and practises until it 'overlearns' the movements, passing the newly acquired information to the subconscious mind for automatic control in the future.

Movements and physiological changes are not the only responsibilities of your subconscious mind. Some of your thoughts and feelings also occur in this domain. Often you think a negative thought without being consciously aware of it. This may explain why sometimes you feel depressed or sad without any apparent reason for feeling this way. You may be surprised to learn that the average person thinks about 50,000 thoughts a day! Even more surprising is that negative thoughts (both about ourselves and others) make up sixty per cent of this number. A study in the United States that monitored the verbal behaviour of a number of parents found that in a given day each parent directed towards their children an average of 400 negative statements (as compared to only thirty positive statements).

Such a bombardment of negative statements can have a tremendous effect on our way of dealing with stress. Children, even more than adults, tend to believe their own bad press. Worse, they tend to follow their parents' example. As adults, they blame themselves too often for mishaps or circumstances beyond their control. And negative self-talk gives rise to negative emotions.

But you can stem the tide of your own negative thoughts. First, you need to recognize that they are *your* thoughts. No one *makes* you think badly about yourself. Whenever you catch yourself talking negatively to yourself, say (out loud or in your own mind) 'Stop! Cancel! Cancel!' Then replace the negative self-talk with positive expressions. For example, if your self-talk before an interview is 'My heart is speeding. I must be nervous. I know I'm going to mess this up', you can replace this flow of negative comment with 'My heart is speeding. I must be keyed up for this interview. This is going to be the best interview I've ever had.' This is just one example. Use your imagination and creativity to replace your negative thoughts with positive ones.

Another way to fight your negative thoughts is to allow yourself little interludes of positive self-talk. I call this technique 'mirror talking'. If you need to boost your self-esteem, stand in front of a mirror and check your posture (shoulders back, head up, smiling and breathing evenly). Maintaining that posture, say five to ten positive things about yourself. You can say to yourself such things as:

'I like myself.'
'This is going to be a good day.'
'In a stressful situation, I take a deep breath and choose to
    remain calm.'
'No matter what others say to me, I'm a worthwhile person.'
'I'm in charge of my emotions. I choose to feel sad or happy.'

Once I explained this 'mirror talking' in one of my workshops. One of the participants commented that mirror talking and positive self-talk might turn him into an 'egotistic person'. This is a valid comment. There is a possibility that you could become egotistic if you *lie* to yourself. If you know you are obviously overweight, don't stand in front of a mirror and say, 'I like my slim body', or, returning from a meeting where your idea was rejected, don't say, 'I was the only intelligent person in that meeting'. This is not positive self-talk, this is self-deception. But you can say, 'I'm overweight. I'm going to change my diet and begin exercising. I'm going to lose that excess fat. Meanwhile, if people treat me differently because of my weight, that's *their* problem. I like myself and

I'm a worthwhile person.' Or you can say, 'At the meeting they rejected my *idea*, not me. I'm still a worthwhile person.' To raise your self-esteem, try this exercise for three weeks or so and notice the difference in the way you feel about yourself.

a peaceful trip

We explained that, in terms of your emotional and physical reactions, there isn't much difference between actually doing something and vividly imagining you are doing it. You can reap many of the benefits of a warm, sunny day at the beach just by imagining you are there.

The following is an example of such an imaginary 'trip'. To take this 'trip' you need a person to read the script to you, or you could record it onto a cassette and play it back to yourself. Read the script slowly and pause for three to five seconds at the pause markings. You can combine this trip with a relaxation exercise incorporating autogenic suggestion, or you can do a complete body stretch and then listen to the 'peaceful trip'.

Make yourself comfortable. You might even dim the lights and have some soothing music playing in the background. At the end of this session, allow plenty of time to reorient yourself. Now, let's begin our 'trip'.

You are calmly listening to this voice, feeling the sensations of your body . . . seeing the colours around you . . . and becoming aware of your breathing, taking a deep breath and exhaling slowly. . . . As you listen to the sounds around you . . . you become aware of the temperature in your hands . . . and feel relaxed . . . you can keep your eyes open or close them now . . . it really doesn't matter whether you keep your eyes open or close them, because you can still see the shades of colours . . . and you feel the muscles around your eyes becoming very relaxed . . . warm . . . and relaxed. . . . You feel as relaxed as if you were standing on a patio facing the beach. . . . As you gaze into the clear blue sky, you see the seagulls flying in the distance . . . you see the white crystal sand . . . and hear the waves splashing on the shore. . . . As you look closer you notice the steps in front of you leading down to the beach . . . in a moment you are going to walk down these

---

steps . . . when your feet touch the warm sand, they will become completely relaxed. . . . With each step you gradually become more comfortable and more relaxed. . . . You can also see the numbers painted on each step. . . . There are ten steps and you begin from number ten at the top. . . .

Now begin at ten . . . feeling at ease and comfortable . . . as you step on number nine . . . your mind can drift away allowing you to let go . . . eight . . . down another step, relaxing your tongue . . . your mouth . . . and your jaw . . . allowing your cheeks to relax . . . seven . . . your shoulders are loose and relaxed . . . six . . . your breathing is deeper and slower . . . five . . . by taking each step, you become more relaxed . . . feeling secure . . . safe . . . and serene . . . four . . . your arms feel warmer and relaxed . . . as you reach step number three . . . your hands become warmer . . . and you feel a tingling sensation in your fingers and hands . . . two . . . your legs feel comfortable and warm. . . . As you take the last step, your feet become warm and relaxed . . . as they touch the warm sand you find yourself on the beach. . . .

Looking at the crystal clear blue water, you can feel the warm sand beneath your feet . . . as you begin to walk, you hear the waves lapping along the shore . . . smelling the clean air . . . and tasting the salt on your lips . . . you feel at peace and relaxed. . . . You notice a small fluffy cloud drifting in the sky. . . gently and slowly. . . . The sand is warm and you lie down . . . letting go as your body touches the warm sand . . . as your body sinks into the clean warm sand, a gentle breeze floats over you. . . the breeze begins circling your toes . . . you feel its warmth and enjoy the tingling sensation as it circles your feet . . . your legs . . . your pelvis . . . your stomach . . . your chest . . . your neck . . . your mouth . . . as soon as the warm breeze touches your face, your eyes feel warm and heavy . . . making you aware that your body, from head to toe, is going deeper and deeper into total relaxation. . . . As you listen to the sounds of the ocean . . . all the muscles in your body are loose and relaxed. . . .

And you will find that you are able to take this calmness . . . this tranquillity . . . and this confidence with you in times of stress . . . relaxed. . . . Whenever you are faced with pressures, this thought comes to you: 'What can I learn from this situation?' . . . And you are always learning . . . no matter when and where the problems arise, you

> can choose to remain calm and relaxed . . . and respond with creativity . . . a response that shows you are unique . . . there is no human being just like you . . . you are you . . . a unique individual . . . a creative response to stress makes you feel strong and confident . . . that's right . . . you have learned the art of relaxation. . . . Your body and your mind memorize this relaxed state forever . . . whenever you want to experience this state, just take a deep breath . . . and let go . . . you won't even have to think about it. . . . Your response to stress will be creative . . . calm . . . secure and confident. . . . Relax . . . take your time and enjoy . . . that's right . . . enjoy. . . .
>
> Whenever you are ready, you can take five deep breaths, stretch and open your eyes. When you open your eyes, you will feel refreshed, alert and full of energy. You will also find yourself in a very good mood. (If you do this exercise at bedtime, replace the last two sentences with: 'Tonight you will sleep soundly. When you wake up in the morning, you will be refreshed, alert, energized and cheerful.')

The quality of the voice of the narrator plays a crucial role in creating a relaxed state. A calm and soothing voice will help you relax and, sometimes, to fall asleep. Remember that it is OK to fall asleep during such imagery training. *Just let go and enjoy what happens.* As you practise and listen to this script, relaxing becomes effortless and rapid. Practise and enjoy!

reframing

> A Middle Eastern king had a dream. He dreamt that all his teeth fell out, one after the other. Very upset about this, he summoned his dream interpreter. The man listened with great concern to the king's account of his dream and said to him, 'Your majesty, I have bad news for you. Just as you lost all your teeth, you will lose all of your family, one after another.' This sad interpretation aroused the king's rage. The dream interpreter, who had nothing better to offer, was thrown into jail at the king's command. He summoned a different dream interpreter. The second man heard him tell his dream and said, 'Your majesty, I have good news for you. You will reach a greater age than any member of

your family. You will outlive them all.' The king rejoiced and rewarded the man richly for saying this. But the courtiers were very surprised. 'Your words were really no different from your poor predecessor's. Why was he punished while you received a reward?' they asked. The second dream interpreter replied, 'You are right, we both interpreted the dream in the same way. But the important thing is not only what you say, but how you say it.'

The meaning of any event depends on its context. Knowing that your loved ones will die before you may be difficult to accommodate emotionally. But a shift in your perceptual frame, to the positive thought that you will have a long life, diminishes your distress. In this way your mental reframing of a situation allows you to reconsider your reaction to it.

Some time ago I went to the island of Tenerife for a conference. I arrived at the hotel around two o'clock in the morning, presented myself to the receptionist and asked for the keys to my room. To my surprise, the receptionist replied that there was no 'Mr Rowshan' in the reservation list, so I asked him to give me whatever room they had available for the night.

I took my key and hurried upstairs, to a generous suite with a large window. Moments later, however, I realized that I had been given a noisy room facing a highway. I could hear every car as it sped by. But I was too tired to call the receptionist and complain, so I chose to put up with the noise. Needless to say, I didn't sleep well that night; all night long I was aware of the continual sound of cars zooming by my window.

In the morning the sunlight woke me up. When I opened the curtains, I was surprised to discover that my balcony overlooked the ocean. It was an enchanting scene. There was no busy highway at all! There was a beautiful view out over the sea and I could hear the continuous sound of waves breaking on the beach. For ten minutes I stood there mesmerized by the sight and sound of the Atlantic Ocean. The next night I slept well, because I love the relaxing, rhythmic sound of ocean waves.

Notice how my assumptions had distorted reality. When I assumed that the sounds I was hearing were those of a busy highway, I framed the experience as unpleasant and suffered accordingly. The next night,

I heard the same sound but framed it differently, changing my whole reaction to it to one of pleasure. This is the power of reframing.

Let me illustrate the power of reframing with another story. Some years ago at my brother's wedding in Canada I was called to help a young man. My sister said that one of her friends, let's call him Tom, was having a panic attack. On the way to the hotel room my sister explained Tom's recent horrible experience. Several nights previously, Tom and his friend were racing on a highway. As they were enjoying their high-speed drive in their sports cars, Tom's friend lost control of his car and crashed. When Tom arrived at the scene, he saw the battered, dead body lying in a pool of blood. After that tragic accident, Tom began having panic attacks every night at approximately the same time that the crash took place.

When I got to his room, Tom was shaking in the arms of a friend. He had no colour in his face. He looked as if he had seen a ghost – and that was indeed the case. He said that every night at about seven o'clock in the evening his friend's ghost would come to haunt him. Tom was sure that the ghost would 'grab and squeeze' his heart all night, and that the ghost wanted to take him away. Looking at Tom, I judged that his situation was critical.

I had to do something. I assured him that I too felt the presence of the ghost. 'Your friend is *not* here to take you away or harm you in any way. Rather, he is here because he needs your help and prayers.' I continued, 'Your friend, Tom, was a very young person. His death was too sudden and tragic. Maybe he wasn't ready to die. He is reaching out for your help. You can ease his pain.'

Tom was listening to me with great interest. I then asked him, 'Are you willing to help your friend and ease his pain?' Tom nodded and said, 'I'd do anything.' I gave him my pocket prayer book and asked him if he believed in the power of prayer. He said that he didn't. So I told him that I was going to say a prayer for his friend anyhow. After I read the prayer, I gave him the prayer book and left.

Next morning Tom was very surprised. He asked me what I had done to him. He explained that after I left he no longer felt the presence of the ghost and slept all night, something he hadn't done since the accident.

STRESS: an owner's manual

Again we see the power of reframing. In Tom's perception, his dead friend was changed from a vengeful, ill-intentioned ghost to a soul desperately in need of prayer. Night-time will now serve to remind him of the need to pray for his dear friend rather than generating fear and guilt.

Do you have any experience in life that you need to reframe? I include here a list of some common complaints that I hear from seminar participants. Try reframing them. Once you have given your own version, you can look at the end of this chapter for other possible ways of reframing these predicaments. Here are some of the most common complaints:

1. I procrastinate.

2. Whenever I'm stressed, I tense up my neck and shoulder muscles.

3. This past year I made the biggest mistake of my entire life.

4. I'm not satisfied with my job.

The assumption behind reframing is that human beings are inherently good and that all human behaviour is useful in some way. Take procrastination, for example. Putting off cleaning the oven may not be practical, but keeping yourself from hitting your child is highly desirable. Once you acknowledge the usefulness of a specific behaviour in another context, you can choose to view it in a different, more constructive way.

Please note that reframing should not become a way of creating excuses for yourself or others. If you procrastinate and reframe your procrastination by saying, 'Maybe the task or the deadline is not challenging enough . . . or I'm not ready. I need additional skills', don't stop there. The purpose of reframing is to allow you to appreciate the positive intention behind your behaviour, and to act upon it. Moreover, relabelling your situation or behaviour shows you that there are other contexts in which the same 'undesired' behaviour *is* entirely appropriate.

These are some possible ways to reframe the common examples given above. You may have come up with different ones; there can be several ways to reframe these examples.

1. If I procrastinate in doing something, it may mean that the task is not challenging enough for me. I'm going to make the deadline tighter.

2. Under stress I tense up. Isn't it great that my body lets me know when I have to relax?

3. I have made many mistakes recently. This means that during the past year I have learned more than ever before.

4. I don't like my job. It's good that I recognize the fact that I deserve better. I can either do something to improve my attitude to my job, or I can change it.

In this chapter I have described just some of the mental skills you can use in times of stress. Practise each of these until you become familiar with them, and you will soon learn which one brings the best results for you.

five

the emotional dimension

Your emotions can heal or wound your body. If you express your emotions constructively, you learn and grow; if you mismanage your emotions, you open the door to a host of health problems. Creative expression and channelling of your emotions plays a key role in your emotional well-being. Here are some resources you can benefit from in nourishing and maintaining your emotional health.

your support system

If you were to lose your job, suffer the breakup of a relationship, or experience the death of a loved one, who would you call? Do you have a person who will lend a sympathetic ear in times of stress? Your spouse, friends, colleagues, or relatives can all be sources of emotional support. And we all need each other.

Talking about our problems is still the best cure for them. A study on the beneficial effects of psychotherapy showed no significant difference between professional counselling and a confiding and trusting personal relationship. Talking out your worries and problems helps alleviate the pain and may even give you an insight into possible solutions. Often just knowing that there are people who support you is comforting.

As with everything else, we sometimes misuse our support systems. We may expect other people to solve our problems for us. We may use our problems and emotions as a means of attracting attention. But if you are open and sincere about your problems, your support system – those who love and care for you – will most likely be happy to come to your aid.

touch

Human contact is vital to our emotional health. By way of illustration, consider the famous case of Anna. Anna was an illegitimate child whose mother, ashamed of her, hid her away. Other than being fed, Anna was given only minimal care. She was left alone most of the time, and when she was discovered, she couldn't walk or talk. Lack of human contact had left her physically and mentally stunted.

We need human contact to realize our full human potential. Physical contact is as important as emotional intimacy; and touch plays an important part in keeping us healthy.

The adrenaline that our body produces during the fight-or-flight response gives rise to a number of physiological reactions. But your body also produces its own natural painkillers, called endorphins. These opiate-like substances, released by your brain when the body is under exertion, ease pain in the nervous system. For example, after a certain amount of jogging, you get a pleasant feeling known as 'runner's high', caused by the endorphins released into your system.

But physical exertion and pain are not the only endorphin triggers. Touch also causes the brain to release these natural tranquillizers. A hug is a good way to help you feel better. Virginia Satir, a noted family therapist, once said that every human being needs six hugs a day to maintain emotional health. How many hugs do you give or get in a day? Are there people you can hug right now? Put down the book for a minute and give them a big hug. Surprise them! Don't wait for special occasions to hug people you love.

humour and laughter

Maintaining a flexible attitude to life helps us adapt to changes and keep our emotional sanity. The best way to banish mental rigidity is to nurture your sense of humour. The ability to see the humorous side of every situation both lightens and enlightens us.

Humour allows us to free ourselves from the limitations of negative emotions. It helps us alter our emotional perspective; it broadens our point of view, opening us to new insights and even wisdom. Humour, by changing our perception of events, helps us see alternative solutions.

One night I dreamt a monster was attacking me. I threw rocks at him and tried to escape, but to no avail. No matter what I did to escape that menacing monster, he became bigger. Suddenly I found myself fighting the monster in mid-air. We were suspended there, holding each other's legs and struggling. All of a sudden, I hit upon an idea: I began tickling the soles of his gigantic feet. The monster literally laughed himself to death and fell from the air. That dream reminded me of the importance of a little humour, and I began to apply the same light-hearted perspective to a larger problem I was faced with at the time.

Laugh *with* others and laugh *at* yourself. When you humorously exaggerate your own shortcomings, you begin to see yourself from without rather than from within, and when you see yourself from this new angle, you are better able to acknowledge your faults and mistakes. Acknowledging them is the first step towards rectifying them.

Accident Reports

Consider these devil-made-me-do-it accident reports from genuine official records submitted to police and insurance companies.

'Coming home, I drove into the wrong house and collided with a tree I didn't have.'
'I collided with a stationary truck coming the other way.'
'A pedestrian hit me and went under my car.'
'The guy was all over the road. I had to swerve a number of times before I hit him.'

> 'To avoid hitting the car in front of me, I struck the pedestrian.'
>
> 'In my attempt to hit a fly, I drove into a telephone pole.'
>
> 'The pedestrian had no idea which direction to run, so I ran over him.'
>
> 'The indirect cause of the accident was a little guy in a small car with a big mouth.'
>
> 'An indirect car came out of nowhere, struck my vehicle and vanished.'
>
> 'I saw a sad-faced old gentleman as he glanced off the hood of my car.'

Laughter also has many physiological benefits. In fact, laughter has been referred to as a 'mini-workout'. When you laugh, your neck, chest, belly and diaphragm muscles get a good workout. Moreover, your body discharges more dioxide and produces endorphins and more T-cells, essential cells in combating disease. Laughter *is* the best medicine. Norman Cousins reported, in his celebrated bestseller *Anatomy of an Illness*, how he helped to cure himself by watching funny movies. He was diagnosed as having a degenerative connective tissue disease. Cousins found that thirty minutes of belly laughter eased his pain and gave him two hours of pain-free sleep.

Unfortunately, only a few hospitals have learned from Norman Cousins' case and incorporated 'laughter rooms' into their treatment plans. These rooms provide patients with a variety of materials (funny gadgets, books, videos and toys) to make them laugh.

I remember when my father was in the hospital I asked a nurse if they had a laughter room available. She looked at me with a puzzled expression and said 'What?!' After I explained to her what a laughter room was, she shrugged and said that they didn't have enough money to afford new facilities.

After I discovered that there wasn't even a video cassette recorder available for the patients to use, I went to the local library, rented a 16mm film projector, and borrowed a copy of the Marx Brothers' *Horse Feathers* along with a collection of Chaplin's best films. My father and I watched the movies and laughed for more than two hours. As a result, he felt better about himself and his illness, and changed its apparent effect on him.

In *Love, Medicine and Miracles*, Dr Bernie Siegel writes about hospitals: 'I've often wondered why designers couldn't at least make the ceilings pretty, since patients have to spend so much time staring at them. There's a TV in every room, but what music, what creative or humorous video is available to help establish a healing environment? What freedom is given to patients to maintain their identity?'

Give the gift of laughter. If someone you know is in hospital, instead of sending a get-well card full of clichés written by someone else, send a funny gift likely to appeal to his or her particular personality. Try a humorous book or a book of jokes, a funny tape of a favourite comedian, or, better still, a hilarious film. It is better medicine in many ways than whatever the nurse is giving him or her to take with that little paper cup of water.

How You Can Tell When It's Going To Be a Rotten Day

Your pet rock snaps at you.

You put your bra on backwards and it fits better.

Your twin sister forgets your birthday.

You put both contact lenses in the same eye.

You wake up with your false teeth locked together.

Your boss tells you not to bother to take off your coat.

Your birthday cake collapses from the weight of the candles.

Your spouse wakes up feeling amorous and *you* have a headache.

You turn on the news and they are showing emergency routes out of the city.

You wake up and discover your waterbed has broken – and then you realize that you don't have a waterbed.

You want to put on the clothes you wore home from the party – but there aren't any.

Your car horn goes off accidentally and remains stuck as you follow a gang of motor-cyclists onto the expressway.

In his moving book, *Man's Search for Meaning*, Dr Victor Frankl reports his experience as a concentration camp prisoner. He writes that, after their arrival at the camp and having been shaved all over their bodies, Dr Frankl and his companions were led into a shower. In the shower, they noted how ridiculous they all looked, and laughed together.

Humour – and the prisoners' will to react to their circumstances in any way they pleased – was something that the Nazis could not take away. Dr Frankl helped a friend to find at least one incident every day to laugh at in the concentration camp. Dr Frankl's sense of humour helped him survive his experiences in the camp, despite all the atrocities he saw there.

Develop your own ability to laugh. Difficulties will occur in your life whether you are happy or miserable, so you might as well laugh and have the world laugh with you. A true sense of humour does not make you callous about yourself or others; instead, it encourages you to regard obstacles as challenges. Confront problems and stress with humour in order to enrich your life.

Use laughter as a tranquillizer that has no side effects. You will feel happy and relaxed if you make a habit of laughing thirty minutes a day. There are many ways you can start your aerobic laughter sessions. You can watch comedy shows and movies, collect jokes and funny stories, or just have a good happy chat with friends.

Poor Planning

Here is another example of a humorous perspective on stress. This bricklayer's accident report was published in the newsletter of a workers' compensation board.

Dear Sir,

I am writing in response to your request for additional information on the accident reporting form. I put 'poor planning' as the cause of my accident. You said in your letter that I should explain more fully and I trust that the following details will be sufficient.

I am a bricklayer by trade. On the day of the accident, I was working alone on the roof of a new six-storey building. When I completed my work, I discovered that I had about 500 pounds of bricks left over. Rather than carry the bricks down by hand, I decided to lower them in a barrel by using a pulley, which, fortunately, was attached to the side of the building, at the sixth floor.

Securing the rope at ground level, I went up to the roof, swung the barrel out and loaded the bricks into it. Then I went back to the ground and untied the rope, holding it tightly to ensure a slow descent of the 500 pounds of bricks. You will note on the accident reporting form that my weight is 135 pounds.

Due to my surprise at being jerked off the ground so suddenly, I lost my presence of mind and forgot to let go of the rope. Needless to say, I proceeded at a rather rapid rate up the side of the building.

In the vicinity of the third floor, I met the barrel which was now proceeding in a downward direction at an equally impressive speed. This explains the fractured skull, minor abrasions and the broken collarbone, as listed in Section III of the accident reporting form.

Slowed only slightly, I continued my rapid ascent, not stopping until the fingers of my right hand were two knuckles deep into the pulley.

Fortunately, by this time, I had regained my presence of mind and was able to hold tightly to the rope, in spite of the excruciating pain I was now beginning to experience.

At approximately the same time, however, the barrel of bricks hit the ground, and the bottom fell out of the barrel. Now devoid of the weight of the bricks, the barrel weighed approximately fifty pounds.

As you might imagine, I began a rapid descent down the side of the building. In the vicinity of the third floor, I met the barrel coming up. This accounts for the two fractured ankles, broken tooth and severe lacerations of my legs and lower body.

Here my luck began to change slightly. The encounter with the barrel seemed to slow me enough to lessen the injuries that occurred when I fell into the pile of bricks and, fortunately, only three vertebrae were cracked.

I am sorry to report, however, that as I lay there on the pile of bricks in pain, unable to move and watching the empty barrel six stories above me, I again lost my composure and presence of mind and let go of the rope.

Sincerely,
Policy Number XYZ98765432

The next time *you* have a bad day, try viewing it from a humorous perspective.

mood management

Nothing is worse than a bad mood, because it takes away your energy and your capacity for tolerance. When you are stuck in a bad mood, other people can't make you feel better. Moreover, your frustration at being unable to escape from negative feelings makes a bad mood worse. And it's something that can affect both your work and your dealings with others.

Physiology

A number of factors can cause a mood swing. You have seen how your own negative self-talk can ruin your mood. Food can also affect your mood, as you will learn in the next chapter. And your physiology has a direct effect on your mood – things like your posture, breathing rate, facial expressions and quality of voice.

Let's do an experiment to show you how your physiology can affect your mood, assuming that you are in a good mood and relaxed, having just read the 'accident report' in the previous section:

1. Drop your shoulders and look down at the floor.
2. Stay in this position for about fifteen seconds.
3. Then come back and continue reading.

What did you notice? Did your facial expressions change to match your posture? How did your feelings change? My guess is that your happy mood probably turned into a slight depression or sadness. Now, while maintaining the same posture (dropped shoulders, head down) try to smile and say 'I feel happy'. Do it now. Did you notice that you had difficulty smiling and saying you were happy in a convincing voice?

Why does this happen? The reason is that your body was in a posture associated with feeling sad and depressed, and this automatically influenced the way you felt about yourself. Have you ever seen a depressed person walking tall, looking up, and speaking in a strong and confident tone of voice? Of course you haven't. It would be almost impossible for someone to feel depressed if she were to smile, look up, throw her shoulders back and speak confidently about herself.

When we are happy, we smile. But, surprisingly, the reverse is also true: when we smile, we automatically feel happier. A group of people suffering from depression were asked to smile mechanically, without feeling. They were instructed to tighten the muscles around their mouths and turn the corners of their mouths upwards. The result? They found it difficult to feel depressed, and many felt immediately happier.

Whenever we feel sad or happy our facial expressions reflect the emotions we experience. But is the reverse true? That is, do facial expressions *cause* feelings? Research reveals that they can. In a study at the University of California, researchers asked a group of actors to produce the facial contortions associated with a number of emotions. The researchers found that, during each pose, the actors' heart rate rose and fell in accordance with their facial expressions.

So put on a smile. Next time you are trapped in a bad mood, check your posture, breathing, voice, and facial expression. If you find any of these aspects of your physiology in an unhelpful state, change them in order to change your mood. Now I am not suggesting that you try to force yourself to feel happy every time you are sad. Each of your emotions has its own time and place in your life. Here I am referring to those instances when you feel the blues for no apparent reason. The cause may indeed not be emotional, but physiological. So smile. Then, just for fun, try a silly grin and notice the difference.

Let's continue with our experiment:

4. Keep your shoulders back, sit up, hold your head straight, smile and breathe evenly.

5. Maintain this posture and say 'I feel sad'.

Did you sound convincing? Not likely. You had difficulty saying 'I feel sad' in that resourceful posture because you were giving your brain two different messages at the same time. Your posture suggested confidence, so your thoughts could not overrule it. Another way of getting rid of 'the blues' is by walking. If you choose walking to cure the blues, keep these points in mind. Keep your head up, look in front of you, keep your shoulders back, swing your arms naturally, walk a little briskly, a little faster than usual, and breathe regularly. Keep up your pace for five minutes. If you try this, I can assure you that your mood will change dramatically. I know it sounds too simple. But do it and feel the difference.

Weather and Light

Weather also influences our mood. Daylight specifically affects our emotional health. At the Help Line of the Distress Centre, we received more depressed and suicidal callers in December than in any other month of the year. Why December? Largely because it is the month of the shortest days and the longest nights, the first month in many parts of Canada to bring severe winter weather. Bright sunny days cheer us up, while dark cloudy days turn us into grouches. Researchers have discovered that sunlight has an impact on the production of certain chemicals in the brain; lack of sufficient sunlight creates an imbalance. For this reason, depressed patients are exposed to sunlight or fluorescent light for a few hours every day. Even light from a pair of glasses with small battery-operated fluorescent tubes attached to the top of the lenses can modify the mood of many depressed patients.

A moderate amount of sunlight is good for your emotional well-being. So get out into the sunlight for a couple of hours every day. During winter or cloudy days, turn on the lights at home. According to light expert Dr John Ott, author of *Light, Radiation and You*, full-spectrum fluorescent light is a good substitute for natural light. He says that the usual bluish fluorescent lighting used in our schools, offices and shops has a negative effect on our health, but the warmer full-spectrum fluorescents can change our moods in a helpful way.

Colours and Sounds

Two other things affecting mood and emotional well-being are colours and sounds. Colours are everywhere; every moment we are surrounded by all the colours of the rainbow in various combinations. Research has revealed that colours have a great impact on our feelings. Bright reds, oranges and yellows energize us, while greens and blues calm us down. Bright reds and yellows stimulate our blood circulation and raise body temperature. Blues and greens – the 'cool' colours – have the opposite effect. No wonder the traffic stoplight is the alerting red and the colour of backstage rooms is the relaxing green. You can make use of colours in your own way to change your mood. In winter and on cloudy days, surround yourself with bright colours: red, yellow, orange and pink. Bright colours in winter may not be fashionable, but if wearing them can boost your morale, it's worth the effort.

Sounds can also affect our moods. We are born with a fear of loud noises. Of course, this is a protective mechanism – our ears were originally developed in a much quieter world. Today's urban world, however, is a noisy place and loud noise can trigger the stress response, since it is often an indication of something harmful in our environment. Our brain alerts us in order to protect us. Loud noises can raise our blood pressure, accelerate our heartbeat and induce any other physiological symptoms normally associated with the fight-or-flight response.

Avoid excessive noise. The best gift you can give your ears is a pair of ear-plugs. Have them handy wherever you go. If you are stuck in a traffic jam where people are frantically honking their horns, put in your ear-plugs and hum your favourite tune. You can also use them when mowing the lawn or vacuuming. Remember, if you can't stop the noise, stop its effect on you by plugging your ears.

But not all sound is bad; music can exercise a beneficial effect over your mood and health. According to Dr Avram Goldstein, a pharmacologist at Stanford University, dramatic music can cause the brain to release the morphine-like substances known as endorphins, mentioned earlier. In times gone by, the harp was played to accelerate the healing process. Music has the power to evoke a variety of moods and feelings. If you want to chase the blues away, listen to your favourite upbeat music.

Listen to music with an irresistible beat whenever you need to energize yourself. The right kind of music can cheer you up on Monday mornings and cloudy days.

Examples of Exhilarating, Invigorating Music

Symphony No. 25 by Mozart
O Fortuna by Carl Orff
Third (Eroica), Fifth, Sixth (Pastoral) and Ninth (Choral)
    Symphonies by Beethoven
'Spring' (from *The Four Seasons*) by Vivaldi
Glorification of the Chosen Victim by Stravinsky
Any waltz by Strauss
The *Star Wars* theme by John Williams

---

love

Many philosophers, poets and psychologists have tried to explain the concept of love, and all of them have found it difficult. Some disagree on the fundamental aspects of this emotion, disputing whether the sentiment of love is a need or a want. But all of them consider it one of the most powerful emotions.

My focus in this book is on the practical principles that can be used for becoming and remaining healthy. So I will not dwell on the philosophical or spiritual aspects of love. Neither will I try to define what love is. Nevertheless, I will explore love's benefits. Let me use a metaphor: Love is like electricity. Few of us know the precise nature of electrical current or understand how it powers a light bulb, but we all know the benefits of this form of energy. We know that, besides its power to generate heat, electricity gives light. Without light we cannot see, no matter how good our vision, so we need electricity, even though most of us don't fully understand how it functions. The same can be said of love.

Love is also a skill. And, like any other skill or art, it can be learned, practised and perfected. It is arguable that a person is not born 'loving', but rather that loving people have learned how to give and receive love, because they have had teachers or models in their lives. They have had the good fortune of being around other loving people.

There are certain prerequisites for students of love, eager to learn this skill. First of all, they must recognize that there is no end to this art, that loving is a journey, not a destination. The process of learning this skill is continuous and endless. The next condition is desire. A burning desire gives energy and fights procrastination in any endeavour. A strong desire keeps the student ready at all times to give with humility and receive with gratitude.

Another prerequisite is persistence. Persistence is the most essential ingredient for any kind of successful enterprise. Once students are armed with persistence, temporary setbacks will not affect their motivation. They love and learn from each experience. In this journey students encounter joy and happiness as well as disappointment and pain. But their desire to learn and grow helps them to withstand the ups and downs of the journey.

The fourth prerequisite is humility. Students must be willing to learn from everyone: no matter how skilled any of us may become in the art of loving, we must remain open and able to learn. We learn from both the young and the old. The humble student can learn from his or her own mistakes and forgive the shortcomings of others.

The last prerequisite is acceptance. Students must recognize the uniqueness of individuals, and respect people not only for who they are but also for what they can become. No matter where a student is on the course of their personal journey, they know that there are always people who are more loving, more spiritual, more sensitive and more intelligent than they are. Each person has a unique combination of these characteristics and virtues. For this reason the student does not compare or judge people's capacity to love.

Loveless Times

The need for love is more evident than ever, and the number of lonely people in our society is enormous. This is partly due to the high price we put on our own independence and privacy; we are afraid to talk to other people in public places. We all seem to suffer from the elevator syndrome: we are all passengers between floors, looking at each other's shoes or staring at the ceiling. If we absolutely must speak, we will say something about the weather.

On the other hand, our magnificent modern technologies have diminished all the distances between us. By virtue of various electronic media, we now live in what Marshall McLuhan called 'the global village'. Our TV sets are our windows on the world, and we live in a village called Planet Earth.

The principle of 'love thy neighbour' is still valid in our global society. We now have two sets of neighbours: one is in our local community and the other is all around the world. Some we see in person, and others we meet through our electronic 'window'. It is time to love both kinds of neighbours. We need to recognize that 'the earth is but one country, and mankind its citizens'. Only through this global vision can we strengthen the bonds among the members of our world family.

After all, even the animal world has a kind of altruism operating within it. There are species that, when a predator is near, will put their own lives in danger in order to alert others. This kind of altruism is a sort of biological law of love that ensures survival of the group, and it is often evident among human beings, too, in times of danger or distress. It is a protective instinct that from time to time serves to keep us out of harm's way.

But this biologically driven love is limited and incomplete. Human beings have the capacity to transcend the bounds of this instinctive kind of love to embrace a spiritual love, an unconditional love. Dr Hossein B. Danesh, in an article entitled 'The Development and Dimensions of Love in Marriage', writes about this kind of love. He explains the concept with metaphors:

Unconditional love refers to that process in which the individual loves others because of their inherent nobility, beauty, uniqueness, and his oneness with all other members of the human race. . . .

Furthermore, all people are like the cells of one body – the body of humanity. In order for the body to survive, there must exist a fundamental unity and harmony on the part of each cell towards all other cells. This unity is a requirement for existence and therefore must take place in an unconditional manner. . . .

Such a love may be likened to sunshine. The sun shines on everything, without any discrimination. However, not everything which is exposed to the rays of the sun is capable of taking advantage of it in the same manner. Under the influence of sunshine both the rosebush and the brambles grow, but each responds according to its nature and the degree of its ability. However, the sun is neither encouraged by one nor dismayed by the other. . . .

Such a level of loving is not easy to acquire and, as a prerequisite, the person needs to be fully cognizant of the nobility and spiritual reality of man, the basic goodness of all creation, and the developmental nature of his love. Furthermore, he must be willing to strive fully towards this achievement, a process which requires both constant diligence and the willingness to tolerate the pain of growth.

Action

How can this vision – of a more loving, united world society – be put into action? Here are a few suggestions of things people could do in their own communities:

- Visit a hospital or nursing home for the purpose of visiting someone who is alone.

- Get to know at least one needy family in your community.

- Talk to elderly people. Make the first contact if they are shy.

- Become an active member of a local charity organization.

- Teach your children how to give and love, taking them along when giving to the poor and helping the needy.

- When amongst strangers, break the ice and talk about something other than the weather. Compliment someone.

- Don't wait for Christmas or special occasions in order to give. Spread your gifts throughout the year. Give something away every day – an encouraging word, a smile, or an honest compliment.

This is far from an exhaustive list. People can use their imagination and make loving others a daily consideration.

Writings on Love

Let me close this section on love by sharing three of the most beautiful passages about love that I know. First, Emmet Fox, in *The Sermon on the Mount*:

> There is no difficulty that enough love will not conquer; no disease that enough love will not heal; no door that enough love will not open; no gulf that enough love will not bridge; no wall that enough love will not throw down; no sin that enough love will not redeem. . . . It makes no difference how deeply seated may be the trouble; how hopeless the outlook; how muddled the tangle; how great the mistake. A sufficient realization of love will dissolve it all. If only you could love enough you would be the happiest and most powerful being in the world.

'Abdu'l-Bahá, in *The Divine Art of Living*, writes about love this way:

> Love is the secret of God's holy Dispensation, the manifestation of the All-Merciful, the foundation of spiritual outpourings. Love is heaven's kindly light, the Holy Spirit's eternal breath that vivifies the human soul. Love is the cause of God's revelation unto man, the vital bond inherent, according to Divine creation, in the realities of things. Love is the one means that guideth in darkness, the living link that uniteth God with man, that assureth the progress of every illumined soul. Love is the most great law that ruleth this mighty and heavenly Cycle, the unique power that bindeth together the diverse elements of this material world, the supreme magnetic force that directs the movements of the spheres in the celestial realms. Love revealeth with unfailing and limitless power the mysteries latent in the universe. Love is the spirit of life unto the adorned body of mankind, the establisher of true civilization in this material world, and the shedder of imperishable glory upon every high-aiming race and nation. (pp. 108–9)

Finally, in one of the most beautiful passages ever written on the subject of love, the apostle Paul places love above all other spiritual virtues when he writes to the Corinthians:

> I may speak in tongues of men or of angels, but if I am without love, I am a sounding gong or a clanging cymbal.

I may have the gift of prophecy, and know every hidden truth; I may have faith strong enough to move mountains; but if I have no love, I am nothing.

I may dole out all I possess, or even give my body to be burnt, but if I have no love, I am none the better.

Love is patient; love is kind and envies no one.

Love is never boastful, nor conceited, nor rude. . . .

Love does not gloss over other men's sins, but delights in the truth.

There is no limit to its faith, its hope, its endurance.

Love will never come to an end. . . .

In a word, there are three things that last forever: faith, hope, and love; but the greatest of them all is love.

(I Corinthians 13)

six

the physical dimension

We have discussed the spiritual, mental and emotional dimensions of stress management; equally as important is the physical dimension. Looking after your physical health can even have the effect of prolonging your life:

---

7 Ways to Add 11 Years to Your Life

American researchers studied the lifestyles of 7,000 people for more than seven years. Their goal was to identify the habits of people who were healthy and lived longer. They discovered that the following seven factors increased life-spans by an average of 11 years.

1. Not smoking
2. Drinking moderately or not at all
3. Exercising regularly
4. Eating breakfast
5. Maintaining a normal weight
6. Eating regular meals
7. Getting adequate sleep

The physical dimension is important mainly because it is the most elemental dimension. Our spiritual, emotional and mental dimensions can only manifest their powers through or on our bodies. Moreover, as we mentioned earlier, the stress response is biological in origin; the fight-or-flight response takes its toll first on the body. The various aspects of our being are interconnected, and if we neglect any, the others will suffer. If we neglect the body, we are courting trouble.

the immune system

The human immune system is far too complex to be discussed fully here, but for the purposes of this book, I will give a simplified account of its functions and the fascinating new field of psycho-neuro-immunology. This is a jawbreaker of a name for a science studying the effects of the mind and emotions over the immune defence system. Without an immune system, we would be like David, the 'boy in the plastic bubble' who was born without an immune system and had to live in a germ-free environment. His food was carefully sterilized. Even his mother kissed and caressed him through the plastic. At the age of twelve, he underwent a bone marrow transplant, but David died from complications following the transplant.

Our lives depend on our immune system. Every minute, our bodies have to fight a fierce battle with many kinds of intruders. Right now in your mouth there are a host of bacteria and viruses numbering more than fifty million. Even your toothbrush is a cosy harbour for microscopic organisms. But don't panic! This zoo of organisms can become damaging when they grow in number far above normal levels, but your immune system is fighting them all the time. For example, your saliva contains enzymes that kill bacteria.

At this very moment there is a war going on in your body. Several hundred different viruses and bacteria are lurking within you, and as you breathe, you inhale thousands of these enemies that float in the air. A ferocious army is awaiting them, however, with over a thousand billion warriors (your white blood cells and antibodies) at its disposal.

The Components of Your Immune System

1. Skin Your skin is your first line of defence. Every day thousands of pieces of dead skin flake off your body, allowing bacteria to be shed. Moreover, your skin produces acids that kill many germs.

2. Mucous Membrane The mucous membrane is a moist membrane that lines nasal sinuses, the respiratory tract, the gastrointestinal tract, the pancreatic systems and other parts of the body. The mucous membrane or mucosa secretes mucus, which acts as a protective barrier against all kinds of germs.

3. Neutrophils When an invader manages to infiltrate the skin and the mucosa, little scavenger cells called neutrophils swallow it. They rush to the site of an infection and begin digesting the enemy.

4. Macrophages These scavenger cells ('macro' means big and 'phage' means eater) engulf foreign materials and devour invaders and debris, including dead bacteria. As soon as these large scavenger cells encounter the invaders, they send for helper T cells. They process and display the antigen on their own surface. Their initial function is like a security guard performing a body search. They locate the invaders' ID and place it on their own back. The sight of a foreign ID attracts the attention of B cells and T cells.

Macrophages have different functions. Some patrol the body in search of intruders. Other types situate themselves strategically near tissues such as lungs and liver to mount surprise attacks on the enemy.

5. Helper T cells When your immune system is alerted, helper T cells begin cloning. They divide and transform themselves into memory cells that can remember the antigen that altered their nature, so that if the invasion recurs, they go off immediately, like coded pistols. Once transformed, helper T cells give off signals to stimulate the production of B cells. Helper T cells estimate the gravity of the invasion and report it to the rest of the army. This role is analogous to the task of a head firefighter who gets to the scene of the fire first. He then informs the crew what to expect.

6. B cells As a B cell recognizes a foreign antigen, it transforms itself into a plasma cell, an antibody-producing factory. Plasma cells can secrete 2000 antibodies per second! Like T cells, B cells act as immunological memory cells, generated during the first encounter with infection. These memory cells circulate throughout the body, waiting to respond quickly to the enemy's second invasion.

7. Killer cells These are recruited by helper T cells. Killer cells specialize in mercilessly killing the body's own cells that have been invaded or have become cancerous. They attach themselves, leech-like, to the enemy. Then they secrete deadly chemicals that cause their victims to disintegrate.

8. Antibodies These are Y-shaped proteins. Once they come out of the factory of the plasma cells, they attach themselves to antigens like lock and key. The antibody binds to the bacterium head first, penetrating its 'horns' into the body of the enemy with its tail hanging out. At this stage, antibodies become the means of destroying the target.

9. Suppressor T cells Once the enemy has been conquered, suppressor T cells signal the army of the immune system to halt the battle.

The army of your immune system is always vigilant and has your body cells under constant surveillance. Day after day your immune system fights battles to keep you healthy.

But this wonderful system is not flawless. Sometimes your immune system attacks the body's own cells, the cells it was originally designed to protect. For reasons still unknown to scientists, your immune system can misread the identities, confusing the 'self' with the 'non-self'. When the immune system turns against the body, we call the dysfunction 'autoimmunity'. Autoimmune diseases range from allergies, rheumatoid arthritis and rheumatic fever to juvenile diabetes and multiple sclerosis.

Stress and the Immune System

Well, I don't get angry, OK? I mean, I have a tendency to internalize. I can't express anger. That's one of the problems I have. I . . . I grow a tumour instead. (Woody Allen in *Manhattan*)

Woody Allen's complaint is not far from the truth. Many scientists are convinced that negative emotions and stress suppress the immune function. The Persian physician Razi (AD 850–923), who practised more than one thousand years ago, recognized the power of negative emotions on the body. Razi once treated a patient's rheumatoid arthritis by helping him express anger.

One of the hormones your body secretes in time of stress is cortisol, a hormone known to suppress the immune function.

The first study to show the effects of stress on the immune system was conducted in New South Wales, Australia, in 1975. R.W. Barthorp and his colleagues studied the immune response of a group of widows. They found that the depression of mourning weakened the immune function of the women in their study.

A similar study was conducted at Mount Sinai School of Medicine in New York. This time the subjects were a group of widowers. Researchers found that the depression caused by bereavement inhibited the lymphocytes (or white blood cells) in their fight against disease. For this reason you are more susceptible in times of stress to common cold and flu viruses.

But there is happy news too, for although negative emotions suppress the immune function, positive emotions strengthen it. Researchers have observed that imagery, relaxation, laughter and caring for others all boost the immune response. Howard Hall and colleagues at Pennsylvania State University showed that self-hypnosis and imagery have beneficial effects on the immune system. They hypnotized a group of people and instructed them to visualize their white cells as powerful sharks swimming in the bloodstream attacking germs. This analogy, of course, is not all that far from what really goes on in the bloodstream. Subjects in the study showed an increase in their immune response.

Relaxation also strengthens the immune function. Janice Kiecolt-Glaser and colleagues taught a group of elderly people progressive relaxation and guided imagery for twelve sessions in a month. The subjects, at the end of the training period, showed an increase in the level of killer T cells.

Kathleen Dillon and her colleagues demonstrated that laughter can also enhance the immune response. They showed a funny videotape to their subjects and measured their saliva samples both before and after the viewing of the videotape. The research showed an increase in the levels of immunoglobin A, a type of antibody guarding entrances to the body. No wonder those who have a sense of humour are healthier and happier.

Can caring for other people have a beneficial effect on your immune system? A controversial study exploring this question was undertaken by David McClelland. He showed a film of Mother Teresa caring for the sick and poor to a group of students. Dr McClelland discovered that the students' salivary immunoglobin A concentrations increased as a result of just watching someone engaged in selfless deeds. This study may suggest that serving other people enhances your cellular immune system. Perhaps this finding explains why nurses in a hospital, who are continually exposed to a variety of viruses and bacteria, maintain their health.

An interesting case, published in the Journal of the American Medical Association in 1981, showed the power of the belief system on the human body. One day a young Philippine-American woman living in Longview, Washington, experienced severe pain in her joints. She visited a clinic where her blood and urine were tested. A physician diagnosed that the woman had autoimmune disease (systematic lupus erythematosus). Following the physician's advice, the woman took prescription drugs to treat the disease. But her condition did not improve. The woman consulted another doctor who confirmed the original diagnosis and suggested more potent drugs to fight the disease. The woman instead returned to her native village in the Philippines, where the village's witch doctor claimed that the cause of her malady was a curse, and removed it. She returned to the United States with no sign of any symptoms. Two years later the woman gave birth to a healthy child.

The human immune system is mysteriously connected with the mind. Although the relationship is not clearly understood, we know that the mind can exercise power over the immune system, and can suppress or strengthen your immunity. You can train your mind through imagery to have a positive effect on your physical health. A guided imagery exercise can be found in Appendix I.

nutrition

The science of nutrition is confusing, and scientists are divided in their opinions about the kinds and quality of food we should eat. A plethora of (sometimes contradictory) diet advice has emerged in recent years, but it is clear that a proper diet increases our resistance to stress.

A complete discussion of different diets and nutritional guidelines is beyond the scope of this book. I offer instead some information and suggestions about foods that may artificially trigger or exacerbate your stress response. I also note some necessary nutrients that are depleted in our bodies in times of stress.

The body shuts down the digestive process in response to acute stress. If the condition becomes chronic, the body uses up stored nutrients, and when the reserves begin to run out, we become more susceptible to disease.

Since the stress reaction is firstly physiological, more nutrients are needed in order for the body to deal with it. During a prolonged fight-or-flight response, three types of fuel are consumed in larger amounts: carbohydrates, fat, and protein. The B vitamins and vitamin C are also depleted. If you eat a balanced diet, you don't need vitamin supplements, but if you skip meals through lack of time or an obsessive drive to look slim, you should consult your doctor about appropriate supplements. I also encourage you to read the chapter on time management and reconsider your standards for physical health.

Consider asking a nutritionist to assess your present eating habits; you may not be getting all the nourishment you think you are getting. A nutritionist's job is to help you formulate a diet that suits *you*. Dr Emmanuel Kersaken of the University of Alabama School of Medicine says that the food we eat has only forty to fifty per cent of the nutritional value that it had when it left the farm!

We are all unique in our individual need for nutrients. An American football player, for example, may need (and eat) in a day what most of us eat in a week! The degree to which we are active or sedentary in our lifestyle is an important factor. A farmer who eats fresh vegetables and fruits and enjoys clean country air has different nutritional requirements from a city dweller who shops for food once a week, breathes the polluted city air, works behind a desk and eats potato chips for lunch.

Certain things that we eat and drink have little nutritional value and place a heavy demand on our bodies, often a demand similar to the fight-or-flight reaction. Caffeine, sugar, salt and alcohol can all trigger or exacerbate a stress reaction.

Caffeine

Coffee is used by many people as a stimulant. Every morning millions of us wake up to the smell of coffee, and drink a cup or two (or more!) to get an early boost. Ironically, the same people often drink coffee later in the day to relax and unwind! But the lift coffee gives us comes at a high price. Caffeine stimulates the release of adrenaline, the stress hormone that heightens our sensitivity to potential danger in order to facilitate emergency reactions. People who drink five or more cups of coffee a day may suffer from irritability, nerve and muscle agitation, and headaches.

If your coffee intake could be producing these symptoms, kick the habit. Don't drink it during your work break; caffeine does not help you relax. If you are really hooked on the taste of coffee, switch to a decaffeinated one. Or you can ease yourself off your addiction by gradually decreasing the amount of coffee you drink. Instead of rushing to the kettle or coffee machine when you need a lift, use your imagination; there are many other ways in which you can make yourself more alert. If you want to become alert in the morning, try a lukewarm shower instead of a hot one, because hot water has a relaxing effect on your body. You can also listen to your favourite upbeat music in the morning to get you going. To get more benefit from your lunch break, try a brisk walk.

Sugar

The White Queen in *Alice in Wonderland* made a wise remark when she said: 'The rule is jam tomorrow and jam yesterday – but never jam today.' Although sugar is a valuable source of energy, too much sugar has a negative effect on your health. Excess sugar causes tooth decay and can lead to malnutrition, for sugar is an empty-calorie food. It lacks protein, vitamins and minerals. Sugary foods can interfere with your appetite for more nutritious food.

It also affects your mood. Although ingesting sugar may give you a rush of energy, it can subsequently crash you into a depression and weakness. Avoid excessive sugar in your diet.

- Replace sweetened soft drinks with fruit juices that contain no sugar.

- Read the ingredients listed on the labels of food products. Sucrose, maltose, glucose, fructose, dextrose, and lactose are all types of sugar.

- Replace sweet snacks like chocolate bars, cakes, pies, biscuits, sweets, and sticky puddings with fruits, grains and popcorn.

- Use less sugar in your tea and coffee. Better still, use none at all.

Salt

Your body uses the sodium in salt to regulate many vital functions. Without salt, you would die. Moreover, your body continuously loses salt through perspiration (your body is always perspiring) and urination, and its supply of salt needs to be replenished regularly. The average person needs less than two grams per day, which is a quarter of a teaspoon. But with our typical daily intake of the salt contained in processed foods, sauces, snacks, potato chips and so on, we already get much more than we need. The average North American citizen consumes five to seven grams of salt a day.

Excessive sodium affects both your blood pressure and your stress response. Studies have shown that people who consume too much salt have a higher continuous blood pressure rate than people who don't. Once the blood pressure is elevated (equivalent to what happens during response to stress), health problems ensue.

Try to reduce your salt intake. Remember that our taste is acquired, and that for the sake of our health, we can re-educate our taste buds. If you think your food tastes bland, use salt substitutes, like dried herbs and spices, instead of table salt. You can also try adding some lemon juice instead of salt. The only time you really need added salt in your food is after a strenuous workout on a hot summer day. Then, you really do need to replenish the salt you've lost through perspiration.

Alcohol

Some people drink because they believe it helps them to deal with stress. Although it is true that alcohol numbs your senses and calms your nerves, the habit can also backfire. A few drinks may help you avoid stress for a short time, but when you come back from your alcohol-induced escape, the source of your problem is still present.

Excessive alcohol consumption damages brain cells, which, unlike other cells, cannot be replaced. Alcohol has no nutritional value, and drinking too much causes the loss of minerals in the body such as calcium and zinc, and vitamins thiamin and folacin. It impairs the freedom to choose the way you act, disturbs sleep patterns and leads to loss of sexual function. Even in moderate drinkers, there is an increased risk of stroke.

Although drinking alcohol can be a pleasurable and sociable habit, you can see that there are many related problems. If you can't do without, do with less.

Smoking

Smoking provides another escape from everyday pressures. For some, smoking seems to relieve stress. Curiously, nicotine stimulates the brain to release endorphins that give you a pleasant, relaxed feeling. Studies have shown that smokers have a higher level of endorphins in their body than non-smokers. But, like drinking, smoking has side effects, and they include increased risk of heart disease and lung cancer – real killers.

Moreover, the nicotine in tobacco is a very addictive drug. Nicotine reduces the size of your blood cells, causing your heart to work harder to pump blood. In addition, the carbon monoxide in tobacco smoke impairs the oxygen-carrying capacity of blood cells.

deep breathing

In Latin, the word 'spiritus' is the same for breath and spirit. The 'breath of life' is the essence of our existence, the definition of life itself. The supply of oxygen and the expulsion of carbon dioxide is vital for the functioning of *all* systems in your body. As you read this book, you are breathing in air at the rate of about a litre a minute. The whole respiratory system – using lungs, nasal cavity, pharynx, larynx, trachea, bronchi, and bronchioles – is controlled unconsciously.

The benefits of deep, regular breathing are many. As an adolescent in Iran I began experiencing chest pain – one of the early symptoms of heart problems. My family was worried until my mother took me to Dr Hakim, who, after a thorough examination, told me that there was nothing seriously wrong. The problem, he said, was with my poor breathing. He suggested that I take fifteen to twenty deep breaths of fresh air first thing in the morning. Three weeks later my chest pain vanished for good.

Later, when I was a bodyguard for two VIPs, I used deep breathing to calm me down and keep me alert. Later still, I taught my Kung Fu students the importance of deep abdominal breathing. We all think we breathe normally, but the fact is that after infancy we lose the natural ability to breathe deeply and rhythmically from the abdomen.

Most of us inhale for two seconds and exhale for one second. This means we are using only half of the air available to us in every breath. The proper ratio should be the opposite; exhale for twice as long as you inhale. This will help the lymphatic system, a network of vessels that carries nutrients from the tissue fluids to the bloodstream, to get rid of toxins.

Besides its cleansing function, deep breathing has psychological benefits. Dr John Grinder, who with Richard Bandler developed the

STRESS: an owner's manual

Neurolinguistic Programming theory of human communication, teaches that by controlling our breathing we can change our emotional state from negative and unpleasant to neutral or positive. It is virtually impossible to succumb to disturbing emotions while you are breathing deeply and slowly.

Just as your posture influences your mood, so do shallow and irregular breathing patterns trigger feelings associated with fear, anger or anxiety. And, just as it is possible to change your mood by changing your posture, you can maintain calmness by continuing to breathe deeply and slowly. Therefore, in times of stress, if all else fails, you should take a few deep breaths.

Conduct a quick experiment. Think of a time when you felt angry or upset. Picture it in your mind and recall what you heard, saw and felt. While you are vividly recalling the experience, notice your breathing. Now take ten slow, deep breaths while you continue thinking about that unpleasant event. Breathe in slowly, exhale gently. Take all the time you need for each breath. Make sure you breathe regularly *and* think of the situation simultaneously. What happened? Were you able to hold onto the same unpleasant feelings? If you repeat this exercise, combining deep breathing with memories of the painful event, you will discover that you no longer associate pain with that past experience. Your emotions are either neutral or positive.

Lastly, let us practise abdominal breathing:

1. Sit up straight or lie down on your back.

2. Relax your shoulders and arms.

3. Place your hands over the area around your navel.

4. Focus your attention on that area. (According to Chinese philosophy, this area is the seat of 'Chi', the body's centre of energy.)

5. Inhale deeply, expanding your stomach as much as possible.

6. Exhale the air, taking twice as long as you did to inhale, pulling your abdominal muscles in. (You can also press gently with your

96

hands on your stomach. Notice that your hands should rise as you inhale and fall as you exhale.)

7. Continue deep breathing in this way for several minutes.

Repetition and practice are the mother of learning. At first, deep breathing seems unnatural. Practise and be patient, and you will reap the benefits. Of course your aim is not to practise deep breathing all the time, but rather to make yourself more aware of the way you breathe, so that when your breathing does become rapid and shallow, you can make the switch into a deep and calming pattern.

anchoring

Did you know that you can have 'buttons' on your body that will instantly trigger your relaxation response? The following technique allows you to 'anchor' feelings to a specific spot on your body. Once you have established an anchor or an association between the feeling and the specific cue, you can recall and sometimes relive the feeling by pressing that spot on your body.

The stress response is triggered by whatever cues we perceive as threatening. According to the concept of conditioning or association, we learn to respond to a range of stimuli without conscious awareness. The great Russian physiologist, Ivan Pavlov, made his serendipitous discovery when he noticed that some of his dogs in the laboratory salivated before their food was presented. He observed that his dogs had associated the sound of the experimenter's footsteps with the expectation of food. His dogs would even salivate to the sound of the door opening.

How does Pavlovian conditioning apply to human behaviour? To answer this question, two researchers conducted a study that by today's standards would be considered highly unethical. John Watson and Rosalie Ryner chose an eleven-month-old infant, Albert, as their subject and gave him a white rabbit to play with. Albert showed no fear of the rabbit. The experimenters then began to associate a frighteningly loud noise with the rabbit – during several sessions, they struck a hammer against a steel bar behind Albert's head as he played with the creature. Since children have an innate fear of loud noise, little Albert cried each time he heard the bar being struck.

After the conditioning period was over, the experimenters brought the white rabbit for Albert to play with once again. What do you think his reaction was? He cried, of course. Little Albert's original pleasure in seeing the rabbit had given way to fear of the animal even in the *absence* of the noise.

This experiment showed that associations play a major role in our lives. We automatically stop at the sight of a red light. As soon as we see someone extending their hand for a handshake, we extend our hand too. If we fast for a day, we still feel hungry at our customary meal-times. Cancer patients whose chemotherapy causes them sickness get sick just *before* their treatment times. Even a suggestion of certain sights, smells or sounds reminds us of previous experiences and triggers a conditioned response.

If we can learn the habit of stopping when we see a red light, we can learn to relax by simply touching a certain spot on our body. Here are some ways to 'anchor' yourself to relaxation responses or any other feeling you wish to have at your fingertips.

Use any one of the relaxation exercises you enjoy. Become aware of your state of relaxation, and experience the moment with as many senses as possible: attend to sounds, images, touch, smell and taste. Once you are immersed in your experience, gently but firmly press a knuckle on any spot on your body. Try another relaxing experience and anchor it to the same spot. This repetition will strengthen the effectiveness of your anchor. You can add more calming experiences to your anchor by touching the same spot in the same way. Once the anchor is established, whenever you are under stress, just touch the spot in the same way and with the same pressure to relive the feelings of comfort and relaxation.

massage

As you know, the fight-or-flight reaction takes its toll mainly on the body. During this process, the reserves of energy are mobilized for action, and if you then perform physical work you use up the extra energy locked in your muscles. But in modern society we follow different rules; we don't jump up and strike our boss for giving us too much work, or run away from our car in a traffic jam. Instead, we must stay with the stressful situation.

After practising the exercises and applying the principles presented in this book, you can both stay *and* flow. Most of us, however, tend to stay and *glow* with rage! If you go through typical stress reactions too often and for too long, your body accumulates frustrated energy and remains tensed. The symptoms of this residue of unused energy are many, ranging from headaches to stiff necks to chronic back pain.

One of the best ways to help your body release the tension is massage. Under the hands of a professional therapist, your body can be relieved of its aches and pains. The most important benefit of massage in relation to the stress reaction is body awareness. After regular massage sessions, your body becomes sensitive to muscle tension, and this sensitivity allows you to relax as soon as you notice that you have tensed your muscles unnecessarily.

Five thousand years ago, Chinese healers used massage not only to create a sense of general well-being, but also to treat many illnesses. The art of massage has survived throughout the centuries to the present day, and today chiropractors, physiotherapists, osteopaths and many holistic healers practise massage therapy.

The Benefits of Regular Massage

1. It improves the blood flow, which increases the delivery of nutrients and removal of waste products from the body.

2. It loosens knotted muscles and relieves muscle spasms.

---

3. It relieves aches in the most vulnerable areas of the body in times of stress (head, neck and back).

4. It creates a state of relaxation and euphoria.

5. It gives a sense of general well-being.

6. It gives you reassurance and love. It reminds you of your childhood when you were often cuddled and caressed.

7. Some massage therapy schools also claim that the proper manipulation of the body promotes good digestion, treats constipation, and helps you release negative emotions.

I invite you to visit a massage therapist. In addition to a massage, the therapist will also give you simple tips on how to sit, stand and walk properly. I remember that my massage therapist once told me that my left calf was unusually stiff. He asked me to pay attention to that area of my leg for a week. Two days later I noticed that whenever I stood for a long time, I would tense my left leg. The awareness helped me to relax this particular muscle as soon as I recognized that I had tensed it.

How often should you have a massage? It depends on how much time and money you are willing to invest. I usually have a full body massage once a month. I also take it in turns with my friends or family members to give back rubs once a week or whenever it is needed. I suggest you visit a professional masseuse or masseur. Those of you who have not tried professional massage are in for a pleasant surprise. Once you put yourself under the hands of a trained massage therapist, you'll be sure to go back for more.

exercise

Our bodies were designed to perform many different physical activities, but today our race for progress and industrialization has brought us machines to do most of our heavy work. For many of us, life is a series of sedentary activities, and we economize on our effort and our expenditure of energy.

But our bodies share a characteristic of many of our machines – if they are not regularly used, they deteriorate. We pay a price for our sedentary lifestyle. Lack of regular exercise contributes to constipation, heart disease, musculoskeletal disorders, and depression.

Here is your chance to get physical. The fight-or-flight response mobilizes your body's resources for action. Through exercise you can release the stored tension in your body.

The Benefits of Regular Exercise

1. It strengthens your heart and lungs.

2. It cleans your body through perspiration.

3. It allows more oxygen to all your organs, enabling them to work more effectively.

4. It burns calories, controls your weight, and helps prevent obesity.

5. It strengthens your immune system, helping you fight common illnesses.

6. It lowers your cholesterol level.

7. It improves your powers of concentration and your memory.

8. It improves your sex life.

9. It improves your self-image and boosts your self-esteem.

10. It stimulates the release of endorphins, the body's pleasure chemical.

11. It increases your stamina and resistance to fatigue.

12. It improves your mood.

13. It builds muscles and bones and helps your body retain nutrients.

14. It lowers your blood pressure.

15. It reduces the risk of heart attacks.

16. It helps you sleep better.

17. A study on healthy adults showed that exercise can reduce hostility by sixty per cent and depression by thirty per cent.

I hope that this list motivates you to begin a fitness programme or to continue your present one. Some of these benefits may be more enticing than others, but who wouldn't want a better sex life, a sharper memory, or a more positive self-image?

People's attitudes towards exercise vary greatly. Some of us agree with W. C. Fields who once said, 'Whenever the urge to exercise comes over me, I lie down and wait for it to pass'. At the other extreme, there are those whose motto is 'no pain, no gain', who become obsessed with physical activity and fail to recognize their own limitations.

Moderation is necessary in all aspects of life. Readjust your attitude to exercise so that you can enjoy it. If you are an obsessive fitness freak, you can afford to slow down. On the other hand, if your fitness programme consists of pushing the buttons on your TV remote control, make the effort to start a suitable programme of regular physical activity before your couch-potato lifestyle leads you to serious health problems. Consult your doctor about the types of exercise best suited to your age, weight and current health.

physical examination

There is no illness of the body apart from the mind. (Socrates, 469–399 BC)

Your body is a sophisticated machine. It needs constant care and attention to function properly. Alas, some of us take our bodies for granted; indeed, some of us look after our cars and stereos better than we look after ourselves.

Visit a competent doctor *and* follow his or her advice. I emphasize that you should adhere to your physician's advice. Studies show that up to sixty per cent of patients discontinue their prescription *before* being instructed to do so, and up to seventy per cent don't follow instructions. Another study revealed that many among a group of patients with glaucoma (an abnormally high pressure in the eye causing loss of vision) who were told to use eye drops three times a day or *they would go blind*, did not do so. Even after such a warning, approximately sixty per cent of patients did not use the eye drops often enough. Even after patients were becoming *blind in one eye*, compliance improved only a little more than ten per cent!

Why are some of us so allergic to good medical advice? Some may be concerned about possible side effects. Others may not be convinced about the benefits of the treatment, and still others might fear the failure of the treatment or have had the experience of unsuccessful treatments in the past.

The situation seems so critical that some health-care professionals have turned to the good old carrot-and-stick solution, offering lottery tickets as rewards for patients who keep their appointments and follow instructions. One clinic asks patients to pay a deposit, which they forfeit if they drop out of the programme.

Sometimes the blame lies on the other side. Some patients maintain that their doctors are poor listeners, or fail to communicate: one study revealed that during an average twenty-minute visit, doctors spent only about *one minute* giving information! Ineffective communication seems to be a major hindrance to health care.

In his book *Head First: The Biology of Hope*, Norman Cousins reports a dozen examples of people complaining about their physicians – not about the treatment prescribed, but about the unproductive patient–physician relationship. The following case illustrates a physician's lack of understanding and lack of sensitivity towards the patient.

Norman Cousins writes:

> One of my young colleagues in the undergraduate faculty complained that she was rebuffed whenever she sought to pursue with her doctor the diagnosis or recommendation he had given her. 'He told me not to

bother my head about such things, that he was the doctor and knew what to do. When I remonstrated with him and said I wanted to discuss some things I had looked up in the medical literature, he seemed insulted by my persistence and told me that if I didn't trust him I should go elsewhere. I said that I didn't distrust him, but that I wanted to have the kind of partnership with him that he had with his doctor. He said if I wanted a partner I should go into business, and that he had spent ten years of his life studying how best to take care of patients, not how to be a good partner.'

Such examples reveal a certain arrogance in modern medical practice. In the words of the Prince of Wales in a speech given to the British Medical Association, 'the whole imposing edifice of modern medicine, for all its breathtaking successes, is, like the celebrated Tower of Pisa, slightly off balance'.

What can *you* do? Look for health-care professionals who smile and make you feel more comfortable; who listen to your worries; who explain, in layman's terms, what the cause of your problem is; who suggest holistic alternatives to drugs (hypnosis, biofeedback and autogenic training instead of painkillers); who explain the side effects of the drugs they prescribe, and offer advice to help you prevent the illness from recurring.

If your doctor does all these things, consider yourself lucky to have found him or her. If in general your physician fails to do these things, look for another one. But keep in mind that perfect health-care professionals do not exist. As the saying goes, 'If all else fails, lower your standards'.

Besides seeking out the advice of competent health-care professionals, you can borrow some books on health, medicine and human anatomy from your local library to help you understand your body, and to make yourself aware of the symptoms of common ailments.

Dr David Smith, an eye surgeon at the Sick Children's Hospital in Toronto, one day saw a little girl crying in the hospital. He asked the child why she was crying. She responded that her mother had told her the doctor would take her eye out when he operated on her. The incident prompted Dr Smith to conduct a study to find out what proportion of parents think that the usual procedure for an optical operation is to remove the eye from its socket and then replace it. A full twenty per cent of the participants in the study were convinced that this was the case. And these respondents were people who had either a high school or a university education. Dr Smith's study reveals how little some of us know about some aspects of medical care.

Arrange to have a thorough physical examination once a year. A thorough check-up usually includes a complete profile of your blood chemistry, urine and faeces tests, and breast or testicle examinations. Remember that an ounce of prevention is worth a pound of cure – and is the best way to avoid a lot of uncomfortable or inconvenient treatment.

Besides regular checkups, monitor your health for the symptoms of common problems. Don't wait for your condition to worsen before you seek medical advice. If you have persistent stiff necks or backaches, consult your doctor. Encourage good communication and open rapport with your doctor by doing the following:

- No matter how sick you feel, smile when you enter the room.

- Walk in with this attitude: *you* are the one most responsible for your own health.

- Get to know your doctor. Ask him or her about medical school, the family, and so on.

- Go beyond the uniform; see your doctor as a fallible human being rather than an automaton who should know it all.

- Don't exaggerate your symptoms. Describe your problem clearly and precisely. Give all the pertinent information.

- Don't expect a cure-all drug. Ask about side effects. If your doctor doesn't know what they are, ask where you can find out.

- Where do doctors go for treatment? Ask yours.

- Do your homework. After the physician's diagnosis, get more information by consulting a medical dictionary.

progressive relaxation

'An anxious mind cannot exist within a relaxed body' is the credo of Dr Edmund Jacobson, who developed progressive relaxation. No truer words were ever spoken about relaxation. If you have tried some of the exercises and mini-experiments suggested earlier, exercises that demonstrate a profound connection between the mind and the body, you will recognize the truth of this statement. It is almost impossible to breathe deeply and be anxious.

Progressive relaxation is a technique for releasing tension in your muscles. As the name suggests, you relax your muscles progressively and systematically. You can begin from your head or your feet and work your way through the rest of your body to rid yourself of tension. Besides helping you relax, this technique increases your awareness of your body.

Progressive relaxation teaches your body to recognize tension. Once you learn to tense your muscles voluntarily, you become familiar with the tensing and releasing process. You learn to have better control over your muscles, and by exaggerating the tension in your muscles, you learn to notice readily when they are stiff. Too often we are so busy that we don't notice muscle tension. Only after we feel pain do we become aware of the tension we are bottling up in our bodies. If it weren't for the pain signals triggered by prolonged tension, some of us might not react at all. But you can learn to catch yourself *before* your muscles really hurt.

This is a very practical technique. Once you have practised progressive relaxation often enough, you can relax anywhere. You can use it during your work break, or while waiting before a job interview, or when sitting through an uninteresting meeting – any time you need to release tension.

First, you need to get comfortable. Find a quiet and restful place and a time when you are least likely to be disturbed (or put a 'Do Not Disturb' sign on your door). Make sure the room temperature is comfortably warm. You can lie or sit down, though I recommend you lie on your back when you are learning this technique.

The Progressive Relaxation Technique

1. Begin with a number of deep breaths. Take two sets of five breaths. In the first set, expand your chest as much as possible, then exhale slowly.

2. Now start the second set of breaths, incorporating the first of the muscle-group exercises outlined below. Take a deep breath, hold it for five seconds, and then exhale slowly and completely. Make sure you exhale for twice as long as it takes you to inhale.

3. Resume your normal rate of breathing.

Helpful Suggestions

• As you tense, release and relax specific muscles of your body, allow 5 seconds for your muscles to tense, 5 seconds to release and 5 seconds to relax.

• During each step, repeat the key words: TENSE, for the first part; RELEASE, for the second part; and RELAX, for the last part.

• Besides repeating these words, you can use images to help you concentrate on the muscles. You might imagine a rope or binding being pulled tight around each muscle, and then being slowly, gently released.

• Make sure that you tense only isolated muscles rather than the whole group together. As you tense a muscle, keep the rest of your body relaxed. In this way your body becomes attuned to the sensation of tension in each particular muscle, making the experience of tension appear very abnormal.

• Every time you exhale, picture all the tension coming together from different areas of your body and then escaping from your chest when you exhale.

• *Enjoy* the sense of ease and relaxation that follows.

Muscle Groups

Allow fifteen seconds for each of these muscle groups in your body:

1. FEET, LEGS, BUTTOCKS
a. Curl your toes downwards.
b. Arch your toes upwards.
c. Point your toes.
d. Push your heels into the surface of the floor, bed or sofa.
e. Tighten your buttocks and lift your pelvis slightly.

2. STOMACH
a. Push your stomach muscles out.
b. Pull your stomach muscles in.

3. CHEST
a. Take a very deep breath to expand your rib cage as much as possible.

4. BACK
a. Arch your back.

5. HANDS AND ARMS
a. Make a fist (one at a time).
b. Extend your fingers.
c. Spread your fingers apart.
d. Straighten your arm.
e. Push down your hands to tighten your arm muscles.

6. SHOULDERS
a. Shrug your shoulders (one at a time).

7. NECK
a. Bring your chin to your chest.
b. Push your head back.

8. HEAD
a. Open your mouth as if to shout.
b. Make faces and exaggerated expressions.
c. Squint your eyes.
d. Wrinkle your forehead.

Other Suggestions

- *Gradually* increase the amount of tension you apply to your muscles.

- Don't use progressive relaxation when you are very tired.

- If cramps occur, stretch the muscle and massage it.

Be patient and practise. Give some time to your body to learn the new exercise, and you will soon be able to conquer your muscle tension. Once you gain confidence with this technique, you can do a tensing and releasing exercise any time that tension occurs.

If you find guidance helpful to keep your exercises systematic and thorough, use a coach or read the instructions into a tape recorder and play them back as you relax.

a good night's sleep

A number of factors play a role in the quality of sleep. Alcohol, caffeine and nicotine can all disrupt your sleep. Caffeine stimulates the central nervous system, keeping it alert. Alcohol, when metabolized by the body, will cause you to wake up during the night. Nicotine is also a potent stimulant.

On the other hand, continued use of sleeping pills reduces their effectiveness, as well as causing certain side effects such as grogginess. I suggest you don't use them. Use relaxation exercises to fall asleep naturally.

Napping

Most of us put off relaxing until the end of the week. But our bodies need continual rest to function at their peak efficiency. The body is like a rechargeable battery; don't wait until you run out of energy before you recharge your body. Even twenty minutes of rest allows your body to recoup its energy. Remember that adequate rest keeps your body refreshed and ready for the challenges of the day.

Sleep researchers differ on the effects of daytime napping. Some argue that naps disrupt your sleep cycle, while others claim they enhance it. I suggest you do your own research to discover if taking naps works for you. Take regular naps for a week or two and notice 1) if you feel more energetic during the day, and 2) if you can still sleep at night as before.

If you don't have time to take a nap during the day, try going to bed earlier at night. A study at Detroit's Henry Ford Hospital revealed that people benefit from an extra hour of sleep at night. People who slept longer improved their attention and vigilance. According to Research Director Dr Timothy Roehrs, 'People appear to benefit from getting as much sleep as they can'.

Winston Churchill once defended the practice of napping by writing that 'Nature has not intended man to work from eight in the morning until midnight without the refreshment of blessed oblivion, which, even if it lasts only twenty minutes, is sufficient to renew all vital forces'.

Here is your assignment: take a nap. Research indicates that between twenty and thirty minutes is the ideal length and between two and four o'clock in the afternoon is the best time to do it. Enjoy the refreshment that a brief nap can bring.

PART

three

the skills of
mastering stress

seven

communicating

Communication is vital to human beings. You need to communicate with people in order to express your feelings and satisfy your needs. A day of your life in which you are unable to say what you need, feel and want might be the worst day of your life. Research shows that socially isolated people are more likely to die prematurely than those with strong social ties.

Maintaining the quality of our communication with each other is essential for our well-being, and Ashley Montagu and Floyd Matson write elegantly about it in their book, *The Human Connection*:

> Human communication, as the saying goes, is a clash of symbols; and it covers a multitude of signs. But it is more than media and messages, information and persuasion; it also meets a deeper need and serves a higher purpose. Whether clear or garbled, tumultuous or silent, deliberate or fatally inadvertent, communication is the ground of meeting and the foundation of the community. It is, in short, the essential human connection.

To establish the right kind of connection with the people around us, we need the right kinds of skills. But before we consider improving our communications skills, we should explore some fundamental principles of human communication.

Communication is a process, a give and take, and it does not have a beginning or an end. Its dramatic nature means that we communicate even when we think we are not doing so. It is *impossible* to avoid communicating, and thus, not all communication is intentional. When you stare at the wall during a boring meeting that drags on well past the time it is scheduled to conclude, you are communicating your reaction, whether you are aware of doing so or not. Your posture and facial expression are a virtual billboard of your feelings.

Let's look at a simplified model of human communication. In any kind of communication, a sender, a message and a receiver are necessary. The sender has to encode a message. Thoughts and feelings must be translated into language or actions understandable to the receiver. Once the encoding is finished, you send your message, using a combination of channels. To the question 'how are you?' you might reply, 'I feel great, and you?' As you say that, you may also nod your head, smile, lean forward towards your listener or tilt your head to one side. Once your message reaches the other person, the same process occurs in reverse. The receiver has to decode the message, interpreting it in his or her own way, and thereby translates your message into feelings and ideas.

Communication is not linear. Sender and receiver exchange messages simultaneously. Consider two people in conversation: though it may appear that only the speaker is sending a message and only the listener receiving one, the listener is also nodding or glancing away or crossing her arms, all of which in themselves are coded response messages. Thus communication is a continuous two-way process.

Communication is also seriously influenced by environment and culture. The physical surroundings affect the quality of your communication. A room that is too hot, too dry or too small affects the amount and effectiveness of any communication made in it. The sending and receiving of messages is also affected by mood, attitude and biases, cultural background and personal history. These factors affect how a message is perceived, interpreted and responded to.

In isolation, words have no meaning. Their meaning lies in their interpretation by human beings. We endow words with meanings according to our own experiences. For example, take the word 'respect'. When your friend demands respect from you, the word is used as a label for a specific experience that he or she wishes to have. You have no way of understanding that experience unless you ask specific questions. 'Respect' means different things to different people. One person might take respect to mean that you look at him when you speak to him. Another may interpret closeness or touching or a certain tone of voice as a sign of sincerity or appreciation. Respect, like anything else, is in the eye and ear of the beholder.

Our communication becomes ineffective when we assume that the labels others use for certain experiences match our own. We all experience the world in our own unique way. To enhance our ability to communicate, therefore, we have to get behind the labels and avoid glib or conventional interpretations of them. If you hear 'I need respect' from a person you have always respected, ask questions. You can ask, 'How, specifically, do you define respect?' or 'How do you know when you are respected?' Much awkwardness and misunderstanding can be avoided when you attune yourself to your listener in this way.

Consider the following argument between a couple. One morning Mary gets out of the wrong side of the bed, as they say. She eats breakfast without talking to John and hurries out the door. John hears a loud slamming of the car door and says to himself, 'She is angry at me again. God knows what's the matter with her.' All day long John thinks about how to retaliate. Later in the afternoon Mary comes home from work. She is in a better mood, only to find that John is not talking to her. 'What's the matter with you?' asks Mary. 'What's the matter with *me*? What's the matter with *you*?' replies John angrily. Mary is confused. 'You just don't respect me', shouts John. 'Please let's not have another argument,' says Mary angrily and walks out of the room. They have dinner in silence. John sleeps on the couch.

What went wrong? Many things. First, John assumed that Mary's slamming the door had a certain intent behind it. Secondly, neither of them is willing to ask questions in order to clarify the other person's feelings, needs and desires. As a result, the vicious circle of blame and misunderstanding entraps them.

What can you do if you are caught in a communication loop that is fruitless or destructive? The best thing to do is what linguists call 'metacommenting', which literally means commenting on a comment.

For example, when you and your friend are quarrelling, you can say, 'Our conversation has turned into a heated argument. How do you feel about us fighting instead of talking?' With such a metacomment, you invite your friend to look at the communication from the outside and ultimately free him- or herself from its adverse effects. Gregory Bateson, an anthropologist who has studied human communication, refers to this manoeuvre as 'reframing'. You 'reframe' unhelpful communications in order to benefit both parties.

how to express your feelings

Emotions are a fact of life. We are always experiencing them, and often express them destructively. Communicating your true feelings is neither simple nor necessarily always tactful. (Would you tell your boss or lover that you are bored in their presence?) Even positive emotions are not easy to express; how often have you struggled with words in order to express love to someone?

We are not good at expressing our emotions because we are taught as children that doing so is 'bad' and self-restraint is 'good'. Do you recall being told that 'boys don't cry' or 'girls don't shout'? Children soon learn not to express their feelings spontaneously.

As adults, social restraints prevent us from expressing our emotions anywhere and in any way we want to. Besides, fulfilling the urge to express every feeling we have would turn us into emotional wrecks; our social norms teach us self-control and moderation. Yet, because we learn to hold back many feelings, we experience stress and anxiety about emotions that could be a powerful source of creative energy – if we allowed them to be.

It is not easy to know when, where, with whom and to what degree we should express what we feel. The first step is to become aware of your feelings and recognize that they are legitimate. If you have difficulty getting in touch with what you feel, you can benefit from the following exercise:

Getting in Touch with Your Feelings

1. Find a comfortable position in which to sit or lie down. Take a few deep breaths and relax.

2. Pick three words or images towards which you feel positive, negative and neutral emotions, respectively.

3. Concentrate on each word in turn, closing your eyes and letting it fill your mind.

4. While thinking of the word or image, and keeping your eyes closed, focus attention on different parts of your body.

5. Beginning with your facial muscles, get in touch with the degree of tension and relaxation in all your muscles, from head to toe. You are not going to relax your muscles; you are going to become aware of your body.

This exercise helps you become aware of your bodily reactions to different emotions. It also helps you recognize that you own your emotions, and can control them. Take the next step, and translate your feelings into words. Use 'I' statements rather than 'you' statements, as Thomas Gordon, author of *P.E.T.: Parent Effective Training*, suggests. If you say, 'You make me angry', you blame the other person for an emotion that *you* own. Moreover, 'you' statements reveal that you are not taking responsibility for your emotions. But someone who says, 'When you forget to feed the cat, I feel angry', is communicating without blaming, and in charge of his or her feelings. The emotions you choose to feel are all up to you. It is impossible for one human being to 'make' another person feel something. Notice also that in this kind of communication you should use precise and neutral words to describe the other person's actions.

anger

Anger is the most common emotion. One study indicated that the average person feels angry ten times a day. We get angry at our friends, relatives, strangers – even ourselves. All human emotions, like the stress reaction itself, have a protective function. They can signal danger, enabling us to prepare in the presence of a threat. The basic human emotion of anger is one of our mechanisms for self-preservation.

People commonly express anger either by attacking or avoiding the source of danger. The 'attacker' expresses the anger loudly and sometimes physically; he or she yells and screams, becomes agitated, hurls verbal abuse, blames and threatens. The 'avoider' suppresses his or her anger, denying it, swallowing it, disguising the anger as something else. The 'winner', on the other hand, reminds himself of the HERO principle and remains calm, perhaps saying the word 'relax' several times to him- or herself, or taking a deep breath.

Here's the HERO principle in action:

Happening John forgets to turn the oven off and the dinner is burnt.
Evaluation 'Is it worth getting upset about this?' Mary asks herself. 'It can happen to anyone.'
Response 'Let's make some sandwiches.' She feels good, remains calm, and avoids getting upset.
Outcome They enjoy the sandwiches.

But the dangerous emotion of anger is surrounded by culturally learned 'shoulds' and 'musts'. Guilt and fear are common reactions to expressions of anger, and as a result you avoid indicating how you really feel.

If you cannot confront the person you are angry with, there are a number of things you can do, as I have already mentioned in my discussion of forgiveness in Chapter 3. You can use mental rehearsal. Visualize talking to the person, and imagine the conversation going the way you want. For example, visualize yourself going through the ABC of 'I' statements. Let them know what they did (A), tell them how you feel (B), and finally, indicate how you would hope they would act in the future (C). Of course you also listen to their reactions.

If you find it difficult to rehearse mentally, write a letter expressing the way you feel. The advantage of expressing your anger in writing is that there isn't anyone to say 'yes-but'. You get to roll with your feelings, expressing whatever it is that you feel you need to say. Remember that you don't have to mail it. Writing a letter helps you release and focus your anger, perhaps even allowing you to clarify your feelings.

Another way of getting your emotions out in the open is to act them out. This technique is used in Gestalt therapy. Try this exercise. Arrange two chairs facing each other. Sit on one chair and say to the chair facing you whatever comes to your mind as you imagine that the other person is sitting there listening to you. Then switch chairs and pretend that you are the other person and speak. Speak and act as if you were the other person, saying and doing what you think he or she might say and do. Keep changing seats until you feel satisfied. You will be surprised how much insight you gain when you play the other person.

Channelling or directing your anger is another useful way of releasing anger, because like other emotions it is a source of energy. Anger mobilizes your body's resources in a way similar to the stress response. Your heart beats faster, your muscles tense up, and you get a burst of physical energy. Instead of using this energy destructively by lashing out, you can direct the energy in creative ways.

One day I was quietly reading a book when all of a sudden I heard the blaring sound of my brother's stereo playing the *Glorification of the Chosen Victim* by Stravinsky at maximum volume. If you know the piece of music you know the tremendous sound to which I was subjected. Soon I became irritated with my brother for not letting me know that he intended to produce an earthquake with his stereo, and I became tense. But then an idea occurred to me. I jumped up and walked to his room, and began to move my arms with force in the air as if directing an orchestra. I also mimicked the head movements of a conductor. When the music finished, I asked my brother to keep the volume down and warn me next time. When I returned to my reading, I felt relaxed and euphoric. I had channelled the anger into a physical activity that was safe and fun, helping me to keep my sense of proportion in a potentially stressful encounter.

listening

A study conducted at Ohio State University showed that, on average, we spend seventy per cent of our waking hours involved in some kind of communication. On further investigation, researchers found that of that time we spend nine per cent writing, sixteen per cent reading, thirty per cent speaking and forty-five per cent listening – the largest portion of our communication time is spent *listening*.

Yet though we all learn how to speak, read and write, few of us learn how to listen. No matter how many communications courses they offer, schools don't really teach us the art of listening. But fortunately the art of listening can be learned.

The Chinese character that makes up the verb 'to listen' is comprised of 'ears', 'eyes', 'undivided attention', and 'heart'. These are essential ingredients for good listening. A good listener pays attention, makes eye contact, paraphrases, asks questions and shows empathy. Listening is not an easy task; in fact it can be hard work. You have to be active, and you must remain focused on the content and not be overly distracted by the delivery. You must be patient and let the speaker finish what he or she has to say.

There are many obstacles to effective listening. The average conversation proceeds at the rate of 125 words per minute. But the human mind can think at the rate of 400 to 600 words per minute, leaving the listener easily distracted.

Another obstacle to good listening is an eagerness to interrupt the speaker. As soon as the speaker pauses to catch his breath, we say to ourselves, 'Here is my chance!' and jump in. Studies show that people's last words bear eighty per cent of the meaning of their communication! Learn to be patient and remain silent. Albert Einstein once said that the secret of his success was $X + Y = A$. X stands for work, Y stands for play and A stands for keeping your mouth shut.

Before discussing some tips on good listening, let's read what my favourite writer, Anonymous, has to say about listening:

When I asked you to listen to me, you started to give me advice. You haven't done what I asked. When I asked you to listen to me, you began to tell me why I shouldn't feel that way. You've trampled on my feelings. When I asked you to listen to me, and you felt you had to do something about solving my problems, you failed me again, strange as it may seem. Perhaps that's why prayer works with some people, because God is silent and doesn't offer advice for fixing things. He just listens and trusts that you're going to work it out in your own way.

---

3 Tips for Good Listening

1. Identify the purpose of the communication. Do you want information? Do you want to be entertained? Do you want to solve a problem? Once you establish your purpose, you will know when you are getting off track.

2. Make sure the time and the place are appropriate for the communication. If they are not, comment on it to the speaker and ask for feedback.

3. Be aware of your non-verbal messages. Don't say 'I agree with you' and shake your head. Be consistent in your speech and body language.

---

conflict resolution

Unclear communication is often the cause of interpersonal conflict. Of course, since we are all unique human beings, we all see things differently; conflict is natural, therefore, and can be beneficial, because gaining an understanding of different ways of viewing the world can be a means to growth. In any kind of conflict we must act creatively and use the opportunity it affords us to tap previously unrealized potential. A game involving communication and conflict resolution can be found in Appendix II.

How do you usually solve interpersonal conflicts?

Do you:

- Avoid thinking them through?

- Blame the other people involved?

- Make them feel guilty?

- Belittle them?

- Want them to obey your rules?

Or do you:

- Give in, in order to avoid scenes?

- Deny that there is a conflict?

- Believe that when people love each other they should always agree on everything?

If you recognize yourself in any of these approaches to conflict, you can benefit from the following suggestions.

First, make sure you know the exact source or cause of the conflict. Be clear about who owns it. If a relative asks you to help her child watch less TV, you do not own the problem. You can only help. It is important to know your position in order to determine how and to what degree you can get involved.

Another important factor is to check with the people involved to make sure that your perception of the conflict matches theirs. Identify the needs of the people involved.

Next, set an appropriate time and place to discuss the problem or conflict. During this meeting, clearly describe your desires. Use 'I' statements to express how you feel and what you need. Then let the other person respond. Listen with your ears, eyes and heart. Encourage the other person to express his or her needs and wants. Be sure to listen and get the whole story. And make sure that each of you makes clear to the other what needs to be done in order to rectify the conflict. Ask, 'What do you need me to do to feel better about this?' Once you follow these steps and establish a comfortable rapport, the solution to the conflict becomes easier to find and apply.

6 Ways to Encourage Rapport

1. Give feedback. If the speaker is right or has a good point, admit it. Compliment him or her.

2. Ask open-ended questions. Instead of 'Do you like your new job?' ask 'How do you feel about your new job?'

3. Paraphrase. By paraphrasing the gist of what you have heard, you let the speaker know that you *are* listening. You will also find out whether you understood their message fully.

4. Show empathy. Put yourself in others' shoes. If the speaker expresses anger about her father, avoid criticizing or admonishing by saying things like 'You shouldn't be angry at your father, after all he has done for you'. An empathetic listener acknowledges people's feelings without judging.

5. Use minimal encouragers such as 'I see', 'I hear you', 'I understand'. You can also nod to let others know you follow them.

6. Pay attention to the content rather than to the delivery.

assertive communication

If you are an assertive communicator, you have the ability to say what you think and feel, to say what you mean and make sure other people understand your message.

An assertive person can say 'no' without feeling guilty. For some people, saying 'no' is akin to enduring a painful operation. People do not want to appear selfish, and they believe assertiveness turns people against them. In addition, we often confuse rudeness with assertiveness.

But assertiveness is not aggressiveness. Although in the English language assertiveness can be taken to mean something similar to aggression, in the behavioural context the two things are not the same. An aggressive person hurts, dominates and humiliates others. But in any kind of interaction the goal of the assertive person is to preserve the dignity and self-esteem of everyone involved.

Whenever we communicate, our behaviour falls into one of three distinct categories: aggressive, passive, and assertive.

Aggressive Behaviour

When aggressive people's rights are threatened, they accuse, dominate, exaggerate, threaten and sometimes act violently. They blow up, thereby triggering the stress response. They want to show who's 'the boss' and who's 'in control' of the situation. Aggressive people say things that they regret saying later. They often get what they want, but always at the expense of others. Alienation is the result.

Passive Behaviour

Passive people stand at the other extreme. They do not express their true feelings. They give up all their rights. Passive people extend a red carpet and invite others to walk all over them. They swallow their anger and frustration, again triggering the fight-or-flight response. They never take responsibility for their own wants and needs. Passive people wait and hope that others will satisfy their needs by reading their minds.

Assertive Behaviour

Assertive people stand up for their rights. They state their desires honestly, and communicate their needs and problems in a firm and polite manner. An assertive person respects the rights of others and defends his or her own rights. Assertiveness is the win–win approach to conflict resolution.

Consider the use of assertiveness skills in this example. One evening I went to see a film. After I sat down in my seat, a large group of young college students sat in the row behind me. They were joking and laughing loudly. As the film began, they continued to be noisy. Since they were sitting right behind me, I couldn't hear the soundtrack properly. After I thought about it for a minute, I approached them this way.

First of all, before turning my head, I raised my right hand. Then I immediately turned around and in a confident voice said, 'Listen guys, I know you are having a good time. Would you please be quiet so that we can all enjoy the show?' I looked at them for a couple of seconds without saying a word. They nodded and some of them apologized and said 'Sure, sure'. About fifteen minutes later they once again started joking and talking loudly. This time I only raised my right hand as I had before. I didn't turn my head or say anything. They became quiet. I did not have to repeat my request. My raised arm acted as a signal to remind them to be quiet.

Let's examine my assertive communication. I took several deep breaths to remain calm and rehearsed in my mind what I was going to say and how I was going to say it. I did not raise my voice. I spoke firmly and politely. In noting that they were having a good time, I acknowledged their right to do so and framed it in positive terms. I opened my request with a positive remark. They agreed with me; they *were* having a good time.

Next, I presented my request. Notice that I framed my request in such a way as to win their support and co-operation. Instead of saying 'So I can enjoy the show', I said 'So that *we can all* enjoy the show'. The former statement creates a competitive environment, but the latter statement makes me a part of their group. They can't oppose their own group.

Another tool I used was silence. After I let them know what I wanted, I remained silent for a couple of seconds and looked at them for a reaction.

9 Tips for Assertive Communication

1. Keep cool. Take several deep breaths to remain calm. Rehearse what you are going to say in your mind.

2. Be consistent. Make sure your posture is erect, your face relaxed, your voice firm and friendly. You can also lean slightly towards the person.

3. Be positive. Put the situation and your request in a positive frame. Instead of saying, 'Don't make noise', say, 'Please be quiet'.

4. Acknowledge the intention of their behaviour. For example, if you are returning a defective product, say, 'I understand that you want to keep the number of returns down. But this iron doesn't work and I would like to have my money back.'

5. Be persistent. Repeat your request *until* you get what you want or negotiate for a compromise.

6. Win their support. Use the pronoun 'we' to create a group. Ally yourself with them against the problem.

7. Paraphrase. Acknowledge comments or requests. If you are invited to go out by a persistent person and you don't want to go out, for example, you can say, 'I understand that you would like me to go to the movies with you. I love movies. But tonight I'm busy. Let's make it another time'.

8. Use 'I' messages. Instead of saying, 'The noise of your stereo keeps me awake', say, 'When you play your stereo loudly I cannot sleep'.

9. Avoid using the words 'I'm sorry' when you say no to someone's request. In the above example of an unwelcome invitation, most people say 'I'm sorry I cannot go with you'. In this context, apologizing is unnecessary; you didn't do anything to necessitate an apology.

Assertiveness is a skill. It can be learned and practised. You can use these suggestions and experiment in different situations. You can also begin with small requests and gradually work up to important ones like asking for more pay or a date. If you need further training, you can contact your local mental health organization or your local hospital for a list of professionals in assertiveness training.

the magic of rapport

The foundation of human communication, both verbal and non-verbal, is rapport. The dictionary defines rapport as 'relation marked by harmony, conformity, accord, or affinity'. Any effective communication between two or more people requires a rapport to be established between them. How often have you had the experience of being 'on the same wavelength' with another person, and felt perfectly connected with them? This is rapport at its ideal level.

Several ingredients make rapport work. Next time you are in a public place such as a restaurant, notice people's body posture. When two people are communicating, if they have rapport, they mirror each other's non-verbal behaviour. For example, if one leans forward, the other person follows within a short time, usually within thirty seconds. A study showed the effects of monitoring people's posture. In an experiment, subjects were divided into groups of two people. The pair was asked to interview someone (who was an actor). The actor had been asked to mirror the postures of only one of the interviewers. The actor was careful not to mimic the person overtly and obviously. The results showed that the mirrored interviewer rated the interviewee more favourably. Moreover, the mirrored interviewer said that he 'identified' with the interviewee.

Studies on attraction have also shown that people like those who are similar to themselves. Such studies confirm the old saying that 'birds of a feather flock together'. We usually like those who have interests similar to our own, people who share our background and attitudes. People like people who are like themselves. For example, when you meet someone for the first time in a social gathering, and you discover that you are on the same wavelength, the rapid building of rapport may be at least as much a result of a conversational topic of mutual interest as it is the result of mirroring each others' movements.

The content of your communication will always be important because mirroring another person's body movements occurs automatically anyway. That's right, you echo other people's movements whether you are conscious of it or not. But this does not mean that you cannot become consciously aware of such mirroring behaviour. Once you know that people mirror each other's body language naturally, you can use this knowledge to establish rapport, all the while maintaining a helpful consistency with the content of your communication.

In order to establish rapport with someone, then, follow these two simple steps: 1) mirror their movements, and 2) use their favourite or key words. To fulfil the first step, just do what they do: if they lean back, you lean back; if they cross their legs, you cross your legs; and so on. People who are new to mirroring fear that the other person will detect this and be offended. If you remain calm and practise following the other person's movements naturally, comfortably, you will find that you automatically establish rapport with them. If you become self-conscious and exaggerate, the other person will detect this and feel uncomfortable.

If you feel uncomfortable about mirroring, try the second step for building rapport. According to neurolinguists, people experience the world through the five senses, but three of these senses – touch, hearing and sight – have the greatest function for most people. We do not rely as heavily on the senses of smell and taste to gather meaning from our experiences. According to neurolinguistic theory, people receive information through the senses, process it in the neural pathways of the brain and express it in verbal and non-verbal language.

Richard Bandler and John Grinder observed in *The Structure of Magic* that verbal language is literal. For example, if you say that you can 'see' your way out of a problem, you *are* seeing a picture in your mind at an unconscious level. They also observed that people generally favour one or other of the major senses (touch, hearing or sight) in their experience of the world. According to their teaching, to build rapport you need to 'speak people's language'.

A simple way of discovering which sensory mode a person prefers at any moment is to pay attention to the specific words he or she is using. The following examples illustrate the phenomenon.

A person who prefers touch over the other senses uses the following type of expressions:

'What you say *feels* right to me.'
'I can't get a *handle* on this problem.'
'I want to keep *in touch* with this.'
'I *feel* good about my job.'
'This *rubs* me the wrong way.'
'That's something I *feel* like doing.'
'I like *hands-on* learning.'
'It's a *heavy* responsibility on my shoulders.'
'Now I can *grasp* its meaning.'
'*Walk* me through this exercise.'
'I have a *solid* faith in you.'
'I have a *feeling* she'll call me.'

A person whose favoured sense is hearing will use the following type of expressions:

'I *hear* you.'
'Let me *tell* you all about it.'
'*Sounds* good to me.'
'*Listen* to me, will you?'
'It's as clear as a *bell*.'
'I want to be *in tune* with what you say.'
'Does this *ring* a bell?'
'I'd like to *hear* from you.'
'Don't give me *double talk*.'
'Can you *hear* what I mean?'
'It just *clicked*.'
'Something *tells* me this is useful.'
'This idea has been *rattling* around in my head for days.'

When someone prefers the visual mode, they will use the following type of expressions:

'Now I *see* a pattern.'
'It *looks* like a good idea.'
'An *enlightening* experience.'
'A *colourful* example.'
'This sheds some *light* on what you are describing.'
'Yes, I can *picture* myself doing that.'
'*Looking* back on it, I can see my mistake from a different
    perspective.'
'Don't leave me in the *dark*. Explain your point.'
'I want to get the whole *picture*.'
'Let me *show* you something.'
'Let's *focus* on this point.'

According to the founders of Neurolinguistic Programming, such language is more literal to us than its metaphorical phrasing would suggest. When we say that we 'have a *handle* on this', we are framing our feelings about the experience physically, as though the issue can be touched and held. When we say 'I keep *telling* myself I have to do it', we are representing our experience to ourselves aurally. If we say 'I can *see* my way out of this situation', we are forming a picture in our minds.

Sometimes people use non-specific expressions. For example, they might say:

'I want you to describe something to me.'
'I liked our experience together.'
'Let me know when you want my attention.'
'I don't understand it.'
'I don't like you doing that.'
'The time we spent together was nice.'

Such statements offer no clues to the person's preferred sensory mode. A simple way to stimulate the speaker to use descriptive words (that is, sensory-based expressions) is to ask, 'How, specifically?' For example, if the speaker says 'I enjoyed our time together', you can ask 'I'm curious to know *how*, specifically, [or *in what way*] you enjoyed our time together'. To answer this question, the person has to give you a specific description or interpretation of that experience. To assume that the word 'enjoy' means the same to you as it does to others is to invite misunderstanding.

To summarize, we know that:

1. Without rapport, communication will not be fruitful.

2. People like people who are similar to themselves.

3. To establish rapport we can either mirror people's body movements or speak their language by using their preferred mode of expression.

eight

organizing

goal-setting

'Would you tell me, please, which way I ought to go from here?'
'That depends a good deal on where you want to get to,' said the Cheshire Cat.
'I don't much care where . . .' said Alice.
'Then it doesn't matter which way you go,' said the Cat.

(Lewis Carroll – *Alice in Wonderland*)

One potential stressor is unrealistic goals. If for example someone buys a book on stress management and expects to learn the skills without practice, he or she will be setting an unrealistic goal! Or a determined smoker may vow to quit by the end of the month; a heavy eater, to lose seventy-five pounds in three weeks; an insomniac, to find night-time bliss by the weekend. Laudable goals all, but unrealistic ones.

Equally stressful is a life without any goal. People without goals are distressed by the ups and downs of life. They waste their energies because they have no goals on which to focus their efforts. Even if such people have a vague idea of what they want to accomplish in life, they may still jump from job to job or change fields of study continually, aggravating an abiding sense of dissatisfaction.

Goals give direction to our lives. Once we know exactly what we want, we can concentrate our resources. They also allow us to make choices. Goals remind us where we want to be in life, and allow us to organize a way of getting there. Goal-setting is the blueprint for life's achievements.

But a goal should also be a journey rather than a destination. During this journey, you become aware of your potential. The founder of Individual Psychology, Alfred Adler, wrote in *What Life Could Mean to You*:

> Nobody will worry, I think, about the fact that we can never reach our ultimate goal. Let us imagine a single individual, or mankind as a whole, having reached a position where there were no further difficulties. Surely life in these circumstances would be very dull: everything could be foreseen, everything calculated in advance. Tomorrow would bring no unexpected opportunities and there would be nothing to look forward to in the future. Our interest in life comes mainly from our uncertainty. If we were all sure about everything, if we knew all there was to know, there would be no more discussions or discoveries. Science would come to an end; the universe around us would be nothing but a twice-told tale. Art and religion, which provide us with an ideal to aim for, would no longer have any meaning. It is our good fortune that life's challenges are inexhaustible. Human striving is never-ending and we can always find or invent new problems, and create new opportunities for co-operation and contribution. (p. 58)

The one benefit of goal-setting that is most pertinent to stress management is that it encourages a more relaxed way of life. Goal-setting also allows you to be prepared for obstacles. Would you get on an aircraft whose captain announces, 'Today I'm going to fly this plane. I don't know where to land. I'll decide on an appropriate place when I see one'? Of course not. The pilot knows not only where he is going but also all about how to get there before he taxis down the runway for takeoff. He knows whether the plane will require refuelling. He knows the wind speed and direction. He knows about forecast changes in the weather. Every detail of the flight is preplanned to ensure the safe arrival of the aircraft.

Identifying your goals in life helps you predict, reduce and manage your stressors. Setting goals and making priorities also brings peace of mind, giving you a sense of organization, focus and purpose, and assists you in the efficient management of your time. If you don't have any goals, you are more likely to feel obligated to say 'yes' to people's demands, to be pulled or swayed by others' desires for, or designs on, you. I'm not suggesting that you refuse other people's requests, but that you know where to draw the line.

Before embracing the six steps involved in goal-setting, you should know what you want. If you have difficulty putting your finger on a specific career or field of study or other purpose that interests you, think about the following question: 'What would you do in life that is so important and satisfying to you that you would be willing to pay people to let you do it?' If you cannot pinpoint your goals, you can contact a career counsellor. These professionals help you identify your areas of interest. Through both aptitude and interest tests you can discover both what you are good at and what you enjoy doing – often, of course, these are one and the same.

6 Steps to Establishing Your Goals

Step 1   Identify your goals clearly and precisely on a piece of paper or write down what you always wanted to be, do or have in life. Let your imagination soar. Consider all aspects of your life. Write your goals under the following categories: spiritual, family, social, mental, physical, career. Add your own categories. Write down your goals in specific terms. 'I want to lose weight' is not a specific goal. But 'I want to lose ten pounds by my birthday' is a specific statement about your goal.

Step 2   Set a deadline. The purpose of dating your goal is to keep you motivated. Without a fixed deadline, you will procrastinate. Imagine a teacher asking her students to write a term paper. She tells them in the class, 'Don't worry about a deadline. Write the paper and hand it in to me whenever you finish it.'

How many of her students will even begin to write the term paper, let alone hand it in? Also make sure that your deadline is reasonable and challenging. If you cannot estimate the time, ask people who have similar goals.

Step 3 Identify the skills you need. Let's say your goal is to become more relaxed and in control of your anger. After writing this goal in specific terms and setting a deadline for accomplishing it, you have to practise and learn relaxation techniques. Find people who remain calm in stressful situations. Talk to them about their philosophy, observe them and model your behaviour on theirs.

Step 4 Anticipate obstacles. This step is important because you can write your goals, set a deadline and learn the necessary skills, but obstacles can always interfere with your plans. If you are not ready to encounter obstacles, you can lose your motivation and soon get off track.

Step 5 Consider why you want to reach your goal. How will reaching your goal benefit you and others? Once you can answer this question and write down the specific ways in which your goal is beneficial, you have claimed it. A reason for achieving your goal gives meaning and adds passion to your efforts.

Step 6 Make a commitment. Many of us don't like the word 'commitment'. We try to avoid it because it brings work and responsibilities. But commitment is the most essential ingredient in setting and reaching your goals. Share your goals with supportive people. Avoid telling your plans to people who would suggest that your goal is 'impossible' or say things like 'you can't do that', 'be realistic, it's not possible for a woman', or 'you are too old to go back to university'. Only talk about your goals with people who offer support and encouragement.

To ensure the successful achievement of your goals, write them out on index cards and read them to yourself daily. Put them in your wallet or purse, stick them on your fridge, or tape them to your bathroom mirror where you'll be reminded of them. You can also nurture your expectations by visualizing the achievement of your goals. Mental imagery and rehearsal have proved to be as effective as real, physical practice. A classic study conducted by Dr A. Richardson showed that mental practice of a sport or activity is as beneficial as the real thing. Dr Richardson instructed a group of people to use only imagery to practise making free throws with a basketball. They did not practise on court at all during the experiment. They just sat and visualized themselves throwing successful free throws. The results showed that this group scored just as well in the real game as players who practised in a gymnasium.

procrastination

Procrastination is the major self-induced obstacle to achieving your goals. If you begin to procrastinate, look at your goals closely. Maybe you are not ready for them or fear possible failure. Maybe the goal is not challenging enough. Or you could be cautious about risk-taking, and fear even successful change. Possibly you think that others will not approve of your goal.

Let's explore the most common reason for procrastination: fear of failure. When a child begins to learn how to walk, her brain stores all her trials and errors in her subconscious mind. Only by trial and error does the child learn which muscles to tense and which ones to relax and in what order. Without error, she will not be able to learn how to walk. Every wrong move she makes is part of the process of gathering information for her subconscious mind. Therefore, the mistakes and failures are essential, because they enable the child to remember what movements *not* to take. No matter what she attempts, the child will always succeed, because she always gathers information about the task she wants to perform, the goal she wants to fulfil.

It is important to remember that failure is a prerequisite of success. Thomas Edison tried 1001 different ways to invent the light bulb.

When he was asked to comment on all those 'failures', he answered, 'I know more than 1000 ways not to make a light bulb'. English novelist John Creasey received 763 rejection slips from publishers before publishing 564 books. You give meaning to your experiences in life. To great people, failure is a learning experience. What does failure mean to you?

time management

Do we pass through time or does it pass us by? Time is a fascinating phenomenon. When we are at ease, time 'flies', and when we are bored, it takes forever. Our perception of time is mysteriously bound up with our experiences of life.

Time can be our friend or our foe. It can be our ally in stress management or a source of the very stress we seek to avoid. Many people feel that 'the faster they go the behinder they get'. They are always late. They don't have a monthly, weekly or daily plan. They don't set priorities. They hop from one activity to another, leaving each unfinished. At the end of the day or week or month they feel guilty and overwhelmed as they find more to do than they can possibly handle.

Before we look at some tips for time management, let's find out how you are doing now. Take a few minutes and fill in a daily time chart. This personal inventory of your time shows you visually how you spend your time during a normal day. You can record how much time you spend on different activities, such as sleeping, getting dressed, eating, shopping, cooking, working, doing chores, taking care of children, and playing.

Once you know how you divide up your time, you will be able to make some changes. For example, you can see if you spend too much time chatting on the phone or watching television.

7 Steps to Effective Time Management

Step 1 Get an agenda or day book to record your appointments, meetings and work schedules. You can also include your goals and objectives. Set priorities, from the most urgent task to the least important. Also buy one of those large, plastic-coated wall calendars on which you can write appointments and erase them later by wiping them off with a damp cloth. Your planned activities will be clearly before you all the time, and if you hang the calendar in a prominent place, the deadlines you mark on it will be impossible to miss.

Step 2 Make a list of things to do. At night, write down the activities for the next day according to your goals and priorities. Place them in order of importance: urgent, important, and 'can wait'. The next morning, do the first item on your list immediately. Make sure you finish it; don't allow distractions to get in the way. Then tackle the next item.

Step 3 Reward yourself. Set realistic deadlines and reward yourself for each task you finish. A reward need not be expensive or time-consuming. A pat on the back in the form of a little positive self-talk might be enough. Say to yourself, 'I did a great job on that – and completed it on time', and then move on to the next item on your list.

Step 4 Delegate. Ask yourself if you can and should distribute to others any of the activities you outline for your day. If there is a task you are uncomfortable with or don't feel competent to attempt, ask someone to do it for you. Outline clearly what you expect from that person. Give him or her all the information necessary to carry out the assignment.

Step 5 Review. At the end of each month, look back on your agenda. See how you are doing and how you can improve. This monthly review will show you your strengths and weaknesses.

Step 6 Watch for time robbers, like procrastination. Remember that you have complete control over your time. Motivate yourself to do things right away. I sometimes put a sign on my desk that reads 'Do It Now!'

Step 7 Get organized. Another little time robber is a messy environment. When you have to shuffle through an endless stack of papers, books, bills, magazines and other things to find something, you waste time that could be spent carrying out the actual task you have set for yourself. If your work area is disorganized, straighten it up. Put things in their place, where they will be handy and easy to find. Do a little spring cleaning every Saturday or Sunday morning. A tidy and organized place to work saves you much time and frustration and makes it easier to accomplish what you want in the time you allot to doing it.

problem-solving

Every day we are faced with problems at work and at home, problems that vary from which restaurant to visit to which house to purchase. The inability to come up with satisfying solutions becomes frustrating. But problems by themselves are good in that they challenge us to tap into our potential. Problems enhance our creativity and help us grow.

In general there are two different approaches to problem-solving. One approach is linear and logical. The second approach is creative, and often called 'lateral thinking'. When you approach a problem logically, you follow a series of logical steps. But in the creative approach you don't follow any logical or orderly steps – quite the opposite, you break the rules of logic and trust your creativity and intuition to tackle the problem. You wander, doodle, shift perspective, investigate from different angles, try different things.

The Logical Approach to Problem-Solving

1. Identify the problem clearly. Some skip this most important step and try to think about the solution without first understanding the problem. Maybe you should write it down, even draw diagrams to help you visualize the difficulty. Maybe you should talk it over with someone. Anything to make sure you fully understand the problem at hand.

2. Set your criteria. A criterion is a standard on which you base a judgement or decision. Knowing your standards allows you to choose the best alternatives. If you want to buy a pair of shoes, and one of your criteria is durability, this criterion helps to determine which shoes you should buy.

3. Brainstorm for alternatives. Once you know the problem and have identified your standards, you begin to come up with as many alternatives as possible. At this stage you try not to judge the ideas. Your job at this point is to think of as many different approaches as possible. Remember that nothing is impossible or out of the question.

4. Analyse each alternative. To do this, list the advantages and disadvantages. Weigh each alternative against your criteria and discard those that don't measure up.

5. Choose one or a combination of solutions. You can either select the most appropriate alternative or take different aspects of each alternative and create a new one.

6. Implement the solution. This is an important step. Often people identify the problem, set their criteria, brainstorm alternatives, analyse and select the best solution – and then fail to specify how they are going to implement it. Decide who is going to carry the decision through, and set a deadline for completing the solution.

The Creative Approach to Problem-Solving

Now let's explore the creative approach to problem-solving. I suggest you try both approaches. I personally find the creative approach more effective and more interesting.

First, we need to consider the implications of our innate urge to recognize and establish patterns. Our brains are designed to distinguish patterns, a process that allows us to deal efficiently with the over-whelmingly large number of stimuli in our environment. This is why we form habits with such ease. As in the example of a child learning to walk, we are constantly making patterns of new sets of behaviours to be stored in our subconscious mind. These patterns are essential in many aspects of our lives; for example, each time you drive your car, you no longer consciously repeat the detailed and laborious tasks involved. Your unconscious mind allows you to drive 'on automatic pilot'. You are able to carry on a conversation or listen to music in your car at the same time as you manoeuvre it about the city streets.

But pattern formation also has its drawbacks, because, in the form of habits, patterns handicap us when we need to break away from them. Although patterns are essential for many of our daily activities, they can also work against our ability to solve problems. Once we form a pattern for perceiving a problem, we fail to see other possibilities for solving it.

We usually rely too much on our logic to solve problems. We like the safety of predictable steps. We often begin processing the problem without considering the role of perception; our perception colours the way we experience the world. We form perceptual filters as the result of our childhood experiences, our environment, culture and education.

Before we can process information logically, we must perceive it. If our perception is distorted or idiosyncratic (which, since we are human, it is) we can get unsatisfactory results. Let's look at our perceptual limitations in more detail.

We live in a busy world. Right now you are processing information that varies from your rate of breathing to the patterns made by the letters on this page, from the shape of the objects around you to the sounds in the background. Since we are constantly bombarded with an enormous amount of information, our brains resort to a number of strategies to simplify our world. According to the Gestalt school of psychology, which emphasizes the organization and wholeness of mental activities, we organize information in certain ways in order to deal with it effectively. For example, we tend to group together items that are close to each other. Therefore we perceive the six lines in Figure 1, for instance, as three pairs.

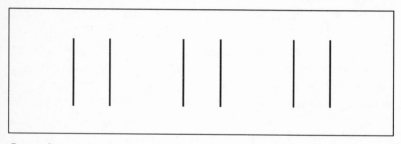

Figure 1

Another way we simplify the world around us is to group things that are similar. In Figure 2 we group black dots together with other black dots and white dots with other white dots. Therefore we see rows in panel A and columns in panel B.

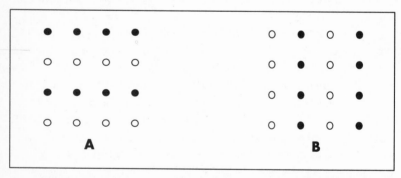

Figure 2

Try the following exercise. Connect all nine dots in Figure 3 with only four straight lines. Don't retrace any lines and don't lift your pen from the paper. Can you do it? Try it now before reading further.

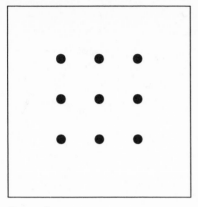

Figure 3

Most people struggle with this problem because the square arrangement of dots creates a mindset or a block for them. The solution is at the end of this chapter.

Another characteristic of our minds is to make assumptions. Read the phrases in the two triangles in Figure 4. Did you notice anything wrong? Most people fail to see that there is an extra word in each phrase. We don't notice it right away because we assume in normal rapid reading that we will see what we expect to see.

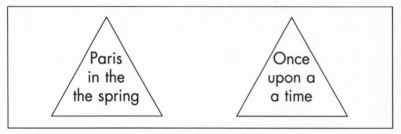

Figure 4

Another of our perceptual shortcomings is illustrated in Figure 5. Can you identify what these shapes are? You will have a difficult time if you see only the black figures – look at the white space around them.

Figure 5

Do you see the word 'fly' now? The reason you don't recognize it at first is because you have been conditioned to read this book by seeing the white page as background and the black marks as characters.

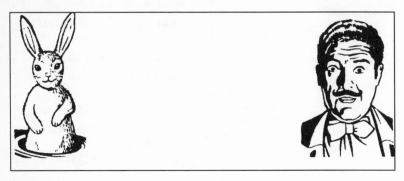

Figure 6

Try one more perceptual observation. Close your right eye and look steadily at the magician in Figure 6 with your left eye. Slowly move the page closer or further away until the rabbit disappears. That is your blind spot. The image of the rabbit cannot be seen because it falls within a small area in the retina that is insensitive to light. It lies in the horizontal plane twelve to fifteen degrees to the nasal side.

Now study Figure 7. Which of the two centre circles is smaller? They are, in fact, equal in size. But the one on the left appears smaller than the one on the right, because of the relative size of the outer circle. Everything about perception is relative.

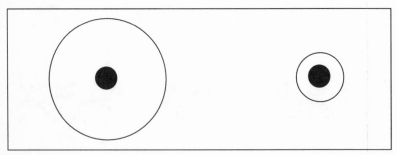

Figure 7

These simple perceptual tests show us that our perception of the world is distorted. Such distortion has a beneficial function in helping us to organize our world, simplifying its complexity and helping us to manage the infinite number of stimuli we receive. Now that you are aware of some of your perceptual limitations, you will be better able to deal with them.

---

8 Tips for Creative Problem-Solving

1. Break free from the logic trap.

2. Challenge your assumptions.

3. Break the perceptual (as opposed to legal or moral) rules.

4. Ask foolish questions.

5. See problems from a child's point of view, or upside down or the wrong way round.

6. Adopt the attitude of play and enjoy all the implications of the exercise.

7. Use stress as your ally.

8. Take risks – have something at stake.

Allow me to illustrate this kind of problem-solving. My father used to own a carpentry shop in the small town of Abhar, in Iran. One day the local bank was relocating and needed to move its safe. The bank was desperate. Everyone in the town had refused to do the job because the safe weighed three tons and was on the second floor of an old building. Not only that, the floor where the safe rested was frail and the movers would be responsible for any damage. No one wanted to take the risk. But my father accepted the challenge and with several of his carpenters went to see the safe. He had to sign a contract guaranteeing that if any damage occurred he would cover the cost of repairs. The interesting thing was that my father accepted the challenge before he found the solution.

Stress was his motivator. He kept thinking about the problem throughout the day. That night before going to bed, an idea flashed through his mind. He discovered the solution. Can *you* solve the problem? How would you move a safe weighing three tons from its standing position on the floor and carry it out? Remember that you would not have any electrical machinery, only simple tools. Remember also that the joists supporting the floor are old and probably rotten. Think about it for a while before reading further.

The solution that my father hit upon involved no danger and little expense. He put several round wooden rods at the foot of the safe. On top of them he placed two sacks of hay. With a lever he tilted the safe towards the sacks, then slowly he emptied the sacks of hay from the bottom. As a result the safe gradually descended onto the wooden rods, ready to be pushed or pulled away. This is truly creative problem-solving!

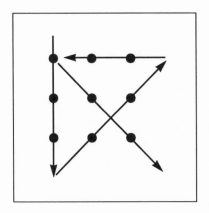

Solution to puzzle in
Figure 3 above.

appendix one

paint a healing image

usually practise the following guided imagery once a week. I visualize my immune system with its army. First I use a relaxation technique (progressive or autogenic relaxation) to release tension. After I'm completely relaxed, I summon the army of my immune system. I picture a vast valley where I meet my white cells. I pay attention to details: colours and shades of things, sounds and smells in the environment, and the feelings I experience. In the meeting I thank my faithful army for protecting my body and keeping me healthy. Then I hug them and give my love to each one of them. After each encounter, they become stronger and healthier. My own procedure isn't very different from one used at the M.D. Anderson Hospital in Houston, Texas, where they use a video game called 'Killer T cell' to help cancer patients visualize their immune system fighting and triumphantly destroying the enemy cells.

Guided imagery exercises are not meant to replace medication or medical care. The purpose of the imagery is to keep your body healthy and augment your treatment programme, but remember that it would be foolish to use imagery programmes as substitutes for medical treatment.

What follows is a simple imagery script that incorporates the well known Chinese principle of Yin and Yang. These terms indicate the two complementary aspects of the unity of the universe. The coloured part is Yin, which represents the feminine, cold, heavy, earth, night and negative principle. The white part, Yang, represents the masculine, warm, light, sky, day and positive principle. Moreover, according to Chinese philosophy, Yin is the human body and Yang is the human soul.

Figure 8: Yin & Yang

Note that although Yin and Yang are divided into distinct parts, they are one. The coloured part, Yin, has a white circle which is the seed of its complementary part. Likewise, Yang incorporates the presence of Yin represented by a coloured circle. Since I refer to it in the script, keep this Yin and Yang symbol in the back of your mind as you read. Then you can picture it when the time comes. Remember also to use a relaxation exercise before this guided imagery.

You find yourself sitting or lying . . . at ease . . . and comfortable . . . feeling relaxed . . . serene and secure. . . . Now you are looking into the sky as you did when you were a child . . . with curiosity and eagerness to learn . . . looking at the stars twinkling in the night sky, filling you with wonder . . . how many places . . . dimensions . . . and realms are there to discover . . . to enjoy in awe . . . and wonder. . . .

At that age . . . you didn't know you were a child of the universe . . . a unique child containing all the beauties and joys of the world . . . you are a part of this universe . . . a limitless universe with its galaxies, stars, planets and creatures . . . all so beautiful . . . so essential to the order of the universe . . . ever-expanding . . . with its dimensions so unlimited . . . possessing potential beyond your wildest imagination . . . to be tapped . . . now. . . .

Eager to learn . . . eager to grow . . . and eager to love . . . experiencing new sensations . . . as you feel relaxed . . . you become aware that your consciousness has expanded . . . embracing new domains . . . new experiences and new learning. . . .

Now you focus awareness on your forehead . . . feeling so relaxed . . . so cool . . . completely calm . . . at ease . . . safe . . . secure . . . letting go. . . . As you feel these sensations, you can see your forehead relaxed . . . and as you look closer, you notice a light . . . gradually taking the shape of Yin, the coloured part of the Chinese symbol . . . gradually you begin to notice the light forming this paisley-shaped part . . . full of light . . . making you relax more and feel the warmth of its rays. . . . For a moment leave the lighted Yin in front of you in mid-air. . . .

Breathing deeply . . . and evenly . . . as you become more relaxed with each breath, you feel your heart beating strongly . . . and healthily . . . you can also see your heart surrounded by a light . . . a brilliant light becoming brighter . . . the light begins to change its shape from scattered rays to form the Yang, the white part of the Chinese symbol of unity. . . .

Breathing deeply . . . becoming aware of your mind . . . calm . . . serene . . . nothing intrudes . . . nothing disturbs . . . you begin to sense the light around your heart . . . as you continue breathing deeply, you become aware that the two parts of the lighted Yin and Yang are coming closer . . . attracted to each other . . . and closer . . . until the two parts meet and become one . . . united . . . forming a round . . . glowing sphere . . . in a moment the sphere begins to hover . . . emanating healing rays . . . touching and penetrating your body . . . making it warm . . . strong . . . healthier and full of wellness. . . .

Sense the healing force . . . its warm rays . . . look at the shades of colour dancing in its rays . . . all the colours . . . red . . . blue . . . yellow . . . orange . . . violet . . . green . . . and all the other colours . . . dancing in the light . . . and you are in tune with the gentle hushing of the light . . . a gentle soothing sound . . . and in touch with the warmth of the light caressing your body . . . enjoy these sensations. . . .

You can see that the sphere glows with white light . . . the Yin, the coloured part of the sphere . . . is full of colours . . . red . . . blue . . . orange . . . and many others swimming in this area of light. . . .

In a moment the glowing sphere begins to float around your body. . . . Now becoming radiant . . . the light emanates its warm and healing rays . . . circling around your body . . . surrounding it . . . feeling so at ease and bathing in the resplendent rays . . . from head to toe. . . .

With each breath you take . . . you become more relaxed. . . as the light touches your toes . . . they become warmer . . . your legs . . . warm . . . the light moving upward toward your thighs . . . becoming warm . . . reaching your pelvic area . . . warm . . . healing every fibre . . . every cell . . . every organ and system in your body . . . your stomach . . . healing . . . your back . . . healing . . . your chest . . . warm . . . healing your heart . . . making it stronger and healthier . . . your arms . . . warm . . . your shoulders . . . warm . . . your neck . . . warm and relaxed . . . moving upward towards your face . . . glowing with good health . . . all the facial muscles are loose and relaxed . . . forehead . . . cool and relaxed . . . feeling a new sense of well-being . . . that envelops your body . . . your emotions . . . your mind . . . and you. . . .

Enjoy the feeling of oneness . . . the healing rays enter deep into every cell . . . organ . . . and tissue . . . energizing them . . . healing any malady. . . . Whenever the healing force encounters healthy cells, its radiant rays transform them into healthier cells . . . whenever toxins come in contact with the healing rays, they just evaporate . . . leaving your body strong . . . healthy . . . and attractive. . . .

The healing force gives you a sense of balance . . . in all aspects of your well-being . . . emotionally . . . physically . . . spiritually . . . you become strong . . . each time you think about this force you become more confident in yourself . . . in your potential . . . and in your power to heal yourself. . . .

If you wish you can also direct the healing light to a particular part of your body . . . that needs special care . . . the sphere of light has at its disposal a beam . . . a vivid . . . penetrating beam . . . just like a flash of light, you can direct the beam on the part of your *body that needs special care . . . special attention . . . special love. . . .*

When the light finishes bathing your body . . . mind . . . and emotions in its healing rays, allow it to return to its safe place. . . . Watch it separate into its original parts . . . you can see them disengage . . . and hear the slight sound that they make at the moment of detachment . . . and feel each one . . . as they return to their seats . . . Yin to your mind . . . and Yang to your heart. . . .

Take your time . . . when you are ready take a deep breath . . . exhale forcibly . . . and gradually return to your fully awakened state . . . feeling refreshed . . . relaxed . . . and cheerful . . . now.

a p p e n d i x
t w o

the prisoner's
dilemma game

The prisoner's dilemma game is a two-player game in which players may compete or co-operate. The outcome of the game depends upon both players' choices. This game is based on a classical story mentioned in *Games and Delusions* by R. D. Luce and H. Raiffa.

A bank robbery occurs. Two suspects are taken into custody and separated. The district attorney is certain that they are guilty of robbery. But she does not have adequate evidence to convict them at a trial; she needs a confession to guarantee conviction. She hits upon a clever plan. She talks to each prisoner separately and offers them two alternatives: to confess to the crime or not to confess. She explains to them that the consequences will depend not only on which option they themselves choose, but also on what the other prisoner decides to do. If they both refuse to confess, they receive minor punishment. If they both confess, they will get intermediate sentences. But if one confesses and the other does not, the confessor will receive a lenient sentence and won't go to jail, whereas the one who remained silent will get the maximum penalty. As you can see, the situation is a real dilemma.

The following payoff matrix illustrates the prisoners' alternatives. As the matrix shows, if they both stay silent they each get only one year in prison. But they have no way of knowing each other's decision. If A confesses while B remains silent, B gets twenty-five years in jail and A is

Payoff Matrix for the Prisoner's Dilemma

Prisoner B:

		Stays silent	Confesses
	Stays silent	1 year for A	25 years for A
		1 year for B	No jail for B
	Confesses	No jail for A	10 years for A
		25 years for B	10 years for B

Prisoner A:

granted his freedom. Conversely, if the situation is reversed, B is freed and A must endure twenty-five years in the slammer. The logical strategy for self-preservation is to confess, since neither of them can know what the other will decide, and if they both confess they will both receive ten-year sentences and avoid the maximum punishment. The ideal answer, however, is to trust each other and remain silent, so that each receives only one year in jail.

As you can see, the logical strategy (to confess) is maladaptive. This scenario shows that sometimes it is better to go beyond our logical, selfish thinking and trust other people. Consider the application of the prisoner's dilemma game to social problems. Negotiations for the reduction of weapons between superpowers, for instance, is a good example of the application of this dilemma. How can one superpower be certain that another will not continue building arms secretly?

Another relevant issue is pollution. Consider the case of five factories, out of which four dump their wastes into a river. If only one factory invests time and money in finding a safe way to dispose of waste, the winners, logically speaking, are the other four factories that dump their wastes into the river without spending any money. Therefore the environmentally conscious factory would be better off, from a strictly logical point of view, dumping its waste into the river too.

The prisoner's dilemma game also applies to our relationships. What would happen if two people in a relationship took the roles of the prisoners in this game? How can you be certain that the other will keep his or her promises? How can you be sure that in any human interaction the other party will follow your mutual goals and interests? The answer to all of these questions is that you don't have any way of knowing. You have to trust others, and be trustworthy yourself; it is the only way.

I suggest you try the following game with your friends, family members and colleagues. It clearly demonstrates the effects of co-operation and competition. Moreover, it illustrates trust and the effects of the betrayal of trust.

The Prisoner's Dilemma Game

This game is played in pairs. The two players are seated apart from each other or back to back, and cannot communicate with each other verbally. Each player needs a score sheet and two index cards, one marked 'A' and the other 'B'.

1. When the facilitator gives the signal, both players simultaneously select one of the cards and show it to each other.

2. Each player then records his or her choice, the other player's choice, the number of points gained or lost (see below), and the total of their points so far on a score sheet.

3. Repeat this process for ten rounds. At the end of the tenth round the players can discuss the game, their feelings, and anything else they wish to mention for about ten minutes.

4. After the discussion, the players play ten more rounds as before.

5. At the end of the twentieth round, the players compare their scores and discuss the game again.

Remember that the object of the game is to accumulate points. The matrix shows the possible combinations. If either player selects 'A' while the other selects 'B', the one selecting 'A' wins 25 points while the other loses 25 points. If both players choose 'A' they both lose 10 points, while if both select 'B' they win 5 points each.

It soon becomes apparent that the best way to accumulate points is by developing co-operation and mutual trust. And in everyday life, applying the same principle is one of the best ways of reducing stress.

Payoff Matrix for the Prisoner's Dilemma Game

Player 2:

		Co-operates (b)	Competes (a)
Player 1:	Co-operates (b)	+5 for player 1	−25 for player 1
		+5 for player 2	+25 for player 2
	Competes (a)	+25 for player 1	−10 for player 1
		−25 for player 2	−10 for player 2

further reading

the nature of stress

Benson, H. *The Mind-Body Effect*. New York: Simon and Schuster, 1979.

Selye, H. *The Stress of Life*. New York: McGraw-Hill, 1956.

the spiritual dimension

'Abdu'l-Bahá. *Some Answered Questions*. London: Bahá'í Publishing Trust, 1964.

Frankl, V. *Man's Search for Meaning*. New York: Pocket Books, 1959, 1980.

Honnold, A. *Divine Therapy*. Oxford: George Ronald, 1986.

——. *Vignettes from the Life of 'Abdu'l-Bahá*. Oxford: George Ronald, 1982.

LeShan, L. *How to Meditate: A Guide to Self-Discovery*. New York: Bantam, 1974.

the mental dimension

Adler, A. *Understanding Human Nature*. Oxford: Oneworld Publications, 1992.

——. *What Life Could Mean to You.* Oxford: Oneworld Publications, 1992.

Blumenthal, E. *The Way to Inner Freedom.* Oxford: Oneworld Publications, 1987, 1997.

Gawain, S. *Creative Visualization.* New York: Bantam, 1982.

the emotional dimension

Cousins, N. *Anatomy of an Illness as Perceived by the Patient.* New York: Norton, 1979.

Montagu, A. *Touching: The Human Significance of Skin.* New York: Harper and Row, 1978.

Ott, N. John. *Light, Radiation and You.* Old Greenwich, Conn.: Devin-Adain Co., 1982.

Sears, W. *God Loves Laughter.* London: George Ronald, 1960, 1984.

the physical dimension

Benson, H. and Klipper, M. Z. *The Relaxation Response.* New York: Avon Books, 1976.

Copper, K. *The New Aerobics.* New York: Bantam, 1970.

Jacobson, E. *Progressive Relaxation.* Chicago: University of Chicago Press, 1938, 1974.

Lappe, F. *Diet for a Small Planet.* New York: Ballantine, 1975.

goal-setting

Clason, G. S. *The Richest Man in Babylon.* New York: Signet Books, 1988.

Hill, N. *Think and Grow Rich.* North Hollywood, CA: Wilshire Book Co., 1966.

Robbins, A. *Unlimited Power.* New York: Fawcet Columbia, 1987.

time management

Lakein, A. *How to Get Control of Your Time and Your Life*. New York: Signet, 1973.

communication skills

Bandler, R. and Grinder, J. *The Structure of Magic*, Vol. I. Palo Alto, CA: Science and Behavior Books, 1975.

Blumenthal, E. *To Understand and Be Understood*. Oxford: Oneworld Publications, 1987, 1997.

Brooks, M. *Instant Rapport*. New York: Warner Books, 1989.

Mehrabian, A. *Nonverbal Communication*. Hawthorne, NY: Aldine, 1972.

Montagu, A. and Matson, F. *The Human Connection*. New York: McGraw-Hill, 1979.

Satir, V. *Peoplemaking*. Palo Alto, CA: Science and Behavior Books, 1972.

miscellaneous

'Abdu'l-Bahá. *Paris Talks*. London: Bahá'í Publishing Trust, 1951.

Alberti, R. and Emmons, M. *Your Perfect Right: A Guide to Assertive Behaviour*. San Luis Obispo, CA: Impact, 1970.

Bodanis, D. *Being Human*. London: Century Publishing, 1984.

Cousins, N. *Head First: The Biology of Hope*. New York: E.P. Dutton, 1989.

Danesh, H. 'The Development and Dimensions of Love in Marriage'. *The Bahá'í Studies Notebook* III, Nos. 1 & 2.

Dawson, C. and Sherr, A. *The Heart of the Healer*. New York: Aslan Publishing, 1987.

Ellis, A. *Anger Management: How to Live With and Without Anger*. Pleasantville, NY: Reader's Digest Press, 1977.

Fox, E. *The Sermon on the Mount: The Key to Success.* San Francisco: Harper and Row, 1989.

Friedman, M. and Rosenman, R. H. *Type A Behaviour and Your Heart.* Greenwich, Conn.: Fawcett, 1981.

Gordon, T. *P.E.T.: Parent Effective Training.* New York: P.H. Wyden, 1970.

Green, E. and Green A. *Beyond Biofeedback.* New York: Dell Publishing, 1977.

Jaffe, D. *Healing From Within.* New York: Simon and Schuster, 1980.

Lingerman, H. *The Healing Energies of Music.* Illinois: Theosophical Publishing, 1983.

Locke, S. and Colligan, D. *The Healer Within.* New York: E.P. Dutton, 1986.

Mendelsohn, R. S. *Confessions of a Medical Heretic.* Chicago: Contemporary Books, 1979.

Murchie, G. *The Seven Mysteries of Life.* Boston: Houghton Mifflin, 1981.

Ornstein, R. and Sobel, D. *The Healing Brain.* New York: Touchstone, 1988.

Paine, M. H. *The Divine Art of Living: Selections from the Writings of Bahá'u'lláh and 'Abdu'l-Bahá.* Wilmette: Bahá'í Publishing Trust, 1973.

Rausch, V. 'Cholecystectomy with self-hypnosis.' *American Journal of Clinical Hypnosis*, Vol. 22, No. 3.

Siegel, B. S. *Love, Medicine and Miracles.* New York: Harper and Row, 1986.

Smith, M. *When I Say No, I Feel Guilty.* New York: Bantam, 1975.

Universal House of Justice. *The Promise of World Peace.* Oxford: Oneworld Publications, 1986.

Weil, A. *Health and Healing: Understanding Conventional and Alternative Medicine.* Boston: Houghton Mifflin, 1983.

index

a

'Abdu'l-Bahá, 83
Abhar, 36, 145
Adler, Alfred, 133
alcohol, 32, 94, 109
Allen, Woody, 89
altruism, 81
anchoring, 97–8
anger, 21, 22, 32, 35, 96, 123, 124, 133: how to express, 89, 118–20
Auschwitz, *see* concentration camps
autogenic training, 56–8, 61, 104, 147
autoimmune diseases, 88

b

Bahá'ís, 3–4, 36, 44, 45
Bandler, Richard, 95, 128
Bateson, Gregory, 116
bereavement, 33–4, 89
blood, 9, 10–12, 19, 47, 78, 89, 90, 95, 99, 105: cells, 11, 86, 89, 95; pressure, 13, 15, 78, 93–4, 100
Blumenthal, Erik, 32

e

f

g

h

i

k

l